the
CDA
Prep
Guide

the
CDA
Prep
Guide

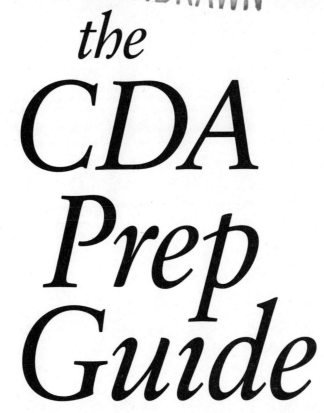

The Complete Review Manual
THIRD EDITION

DEBRA PIERCE

Redleaf Press®
www.redleafpress.org
800-423-8309

Published by Redleaf Press
10 Yorkton Court
St. Paul, MN 55117
www.redleafpress.org

First edition published 2008. Second edition 2011. Third edition 2014.
Cover design by Jim Handrigan
Interior design by David Farr, ImageSmythe; typeset in SabonNext
Printed in the United States of America
20 19 18 17 16 15 14   1 2 3 4 5 6 7 8 9 10

The CDA Competency Goal Standards and Functional Areas referenced throughout the book, the CDA Subject Areas chart in appendix A, and portions of the glossary were reproduced from *The Child Development Associate National Credentialing Program® and CDA Competency Standards* books with permission from the Council for Professional Recognition (www.cdacouncil.org).

The Child Development Associate (CDA) Credential™ is a trademark, and The Child Development Associate National Credentialing Program® is a registered trademark of the Council for Professional Recognition.

The CDA Competency Goal Statements (now called CDA Competency Standards) and Functional Areas referenced throughout the book and the CDA Subject Areas chart in appendix A were reproduced from *The Child Development Associate Assessment System and Competency Standards* (now *The Child Development Associate National Credentialing Program® and CDA Competency Standards*) books with permission from the Council for Professional Recognition (www.cdacouncil.org).

Redleaf Press is not associated with the Council for Professional Recognition. The publication of this book and permissions granted herein are not to be construed as an endorsement for this manual by the Council.

Library of Congress Cataloging-in-Publication Data
Pierce, Debra, 1949-
  The CDA prep guide : the complete review manual / Debra Pierce. — Third edition.
    pages cm
  Includes bibliographical references and index.
  ISBN 978-1-60554-279-9 (pbk. : alk. paper)
  1. Child care workers—Certification—United States. 2. Child care workers—Training of—United States.
3. Child care workers—Employment–United States. 4. Early childhood education—United States.   I. Title.
  HQ778.63.P54 2014
  362.71'2—dc23
                          2013040346

Contents

Introduction

IF YOU ARE JUST CONSIDERING or actually working toward your Child Development Associate (CDA) Credential™, you are to be commended! As in any field, becoming an early child care and education professional takes commitment and a desire to do one's best to meet the quality standards that define membership in a particular profession.

About the Third Edition

In the interest of providing CDA candidates with the most up-to-date help and information possible, this third edition of *The CDA Prep Guide* reflects recent major changes to the Council for Professional Recognition's CDA National Credentialing Program®, referred to as CDA 2.0.

The entire new process is integrated, with each part interwoven with the others in some way, requiring a good deal of reflection—about what has been included in the Professional Portfolio and about the candidate's own philosophy of teaching young children.

With the introduction of CDA 2.0, candidates will create a Professional Portfolio. This replaces the Professional Resource File that had been a part of the previous CDA process. Besides the name change, some notable differences exist. The Resource Collection is still included, and these items are again arranged to align with each of the Competency Standards. However, instead of seventeen Resource Collection items, there are now ten.

Some of the Resource Collection items are similar to those that were collected for the Professional Resource File, but they now appear in different contexts. For example, the candidate will still describe nine activities but is now given specific developmental/learning areas on which to focus. The new Resource Collection will enable the candidate to visit more websites for information, which is a logical change, since the Internet is generally the first place most of us search for what we need.

Candidates will still be locating community resources, such as translation services and agencies that work with children who have special needs. However, these resources will now be grouped together into one section of the Professional Portfolio designated as the Family Resource Guide.

CDA 2.0 also requires that the CDA candidate take on more personal responsibility in the credentialing process. Locating a Professional Development Specialist (also called the PD Specialist) and scheduling the CDA Exam and verification visit are now tasks for the candidate to complete. The candidate will also review the Family Questionnaires that she has collected and will interpret the feedback as it applies to her practices. At the verification visit, it will be the candidate who reflects on her professional strengths and areas for future growth in order to set personal goals and then strategies for meeting them. This new personal responsibility gives the candidate an opportunity to demonstrate the characteristics of a professional in the field—making decisions, reflecting and evaluating, and taking steps to improve practices.

All of these changes may appear to be a paradigm shift, bringing with it some uncertainty and confusion. This third edition of *The CDA Prep Guide* will help you navigate the new CDA process and become comfortable with it, so you can accurately complete the requirements and be fully ready for a successful verification visit.

Pursuing a CDA Credential

CDA candidates have had varying amounts of child care training, through college classes, in-service trainings, or attendance at a variety of workshops. Many are working on a degree or have already earned a degree in a related area of study. Those who are new to the field may have just begun learning about child development and educating young children through their CDA training hours.

The reasons early child care and education providers are interested in pursuing a CDA Credential are as varied as their backgrounds. Some who are already working in the field may need to earn their CDA to retain their positions, advance into lead

The CDA Professional Portfolio is now a resource you can actually use in your work with young children and families. Feel free to continue to add resources to the portfolio after earning your credential.

teaching positions, or become directors. Others who are just enter-ing the field may need a CDA to be considered for a position.

New research, which continues to show the importance of the early years in terms of children's development, offers strong mo-tivation to provide quality care and education in early childhood programs. The only way to accomplish this is to ensure that care providers meet nationally recognized standards in their work with young children.

The CDA program provides the means to assess and creden-tial child care providers on the basis of their work with young children, in their particular workplace setting, with the age group of children they teach.

Aside from meeting mandates or enhancing personal market-ability, going through the CDA process will reward you with confidence and new insight into working with young children. In the process, you will likely gain a sense of personal satisfac-tion in knowing you have the knowledge and tools to do your professional best in your career as an early childhood educator. Completing the CDA Credential is also a great first step in your journey toward continued professional development and lifelong learning.

Regardless of your point of origin—center-based caregiver, family child care provider, center director, or potential early childhood professional—this book will help you understand and complete the CDA process.

You may be in a formal CDA preparatory program or you may be working on your own. Whichever the case, you will be sure to appreciate the easy-to-understand answers, suggestions, and support.

You are embarking on a journey through a series of steps required to earn your CDA Credential. To do this, you will need to complete the 120 clock hours of training, gather documentation, submit the application, take an exam, and participate in the verifi-cation visit with a PD Specialist. When this process is completed, your abilities as a primary care and education provider for young children will be substantiated by this professional, nationally rec-ognized credential, suitable for framing. Be prepared to work hard, learn much, and be extremely proud of your accomplishments.

How to Use This Guide

The information in this book is intended to supplement the materials you have received from the Council for Professional Recognition in *The Child Development Associate National*

Credentialing Program® *and CDA Competency Standards* book. It is not intended as a substitute, nor is it simply another version of it. If you have not, as yet, ordered the *Competency Standards* book, you will want to do so before beginning to use *The CDA Prep Guide*. The *Competency Standards* book will be blue, yellow, or green, depending on your particular setting and age-level endorsement. At the back of each *Competency Standards* book are perforated pages including an Application Form, the Family Questionnaire for duplicating, and the documents needed for the verification visit.

It is assumed that you have completed the required 120 clock hours of formal child care training and are ready to begin the next stages of CDA assessment.

Not every Child Development Associate (CDA) candidate is working in the same setting or with children of the same ages. For this reason, not every CDA candidate will be using every section of this book—only the sections that pertain to her particular situation. Some of the information is of a general nature and is important for all CDA candidates to understand; however, other information is specific to center-based preschool, center-based infant/toddler, or family child care providers.

The purpose of this book is to simplify the required tasks of CDA documentation and assessment into a step-by-step process, whether you are in a formal CDA preparatory class or working through this process on your own. You will appreciate the user-friendly format, helpful suggestions, and accurate information that will enable you to be successful.

Easy-to-understand assistance is provided as you take the following steps:

- Assemble the Resource Collection for the Professional Portfolio
- Compose the six Reflective Statements of Competence
- Distribute and collect the Family Questionnaires
- Select a Professional Development Specialist
- Prepare yourself and your setting for the observation
- Complete the application
- Prepare for the CDA Exam
- Prepare for the verification visit

After earning your CDA Credential, you can continue to use this book to renew your CDA credential, to get a CDA for a different setting, and to decide how to continue your professional development.

Facts about the Child Development Associate (CDA) Credential and Process

What Is a CDA?

CDA stands for Child Development Associate™. This is a person who has successfully completed the CDA assessment process and has been awarded the CDA Credential. She has demonstrated the ability to meet the specific needs of children, work with parents and other adults, and promote and nurture children's social, emotional, physical, and intellectual growth in a child development program. The CDA has shown competence in her ability to meet the CDA Competency Standards through her work in a center-based, home visitor, family child care, bilingual, or special education setting (Council for Professional Recognition 2006, 2013).

When and How Did It All Begin?

The Child Development Associate (CDA) National Credentialing Program® began in 1971, through the cooperative efforts of the federal government and the early childhood care and education profession, as a result of concern about the quality of child care in this country. Throughout the 1960s, a dramatic increase occurred in the number of children in care programs as many mothers entered the workforce, but there was no deliberate and organized effort to keep track of the quality of care these children were receiving. This became increasingly important, as major research studies at the time continued to indicate how critical the care that a child received in the early years was to the child's subsequent development. The purpose of the program was to assess and credential early childhood care and education professionals on the basis of performance. The program was funded by the US Department of Health and Human Services, Administration on Children, Youth, and Families.

For the first ten years, the CDA program was directed by a coalition of early childhood professional associations, including Bank Street College of Education. In 1979, the program added bilingual Competency Standards and assessment requirements to the system, so candidates in bilingual programs could also be assessed.

At first, the program only assessed workers in center-based preschool programs that served children ages three to five. Between 1985 and 1989, the CDA assessment system was expanded to include caregivers in home visitor and family child care programs.

In the spring of 1985, the National Association for the Education of Young Children (NAEYC) began managing the CDA program and set up a separate entity of the organization to administer the program nationally. It was called the Council for Professional Recognition. The Council took on complete responsibility for the program in the fall of 1985. As the result of three years of study and review, the procedures for assessment and national standards for the delivery of CDA training were developed. The Council continues to conduct research on the effectiveness, relevance, and affordability of the credentialing program, periodically making revisions (Council for Professional Recognition 2006, 2013).

Beginning in 2011, the Council expanded its scope as not only an "assessment" organization, but also as an organization promoting professional development, with the CDA Credential as the first step in this process.

In 2013, the Council introduced CDA 2.0. The original Competency Standards and the accompanying thirteen Functional Areas have remained the same, but the procedures and process of assessment have changed significantly.

This new process is much more integrated, with each part relating to the others. It also provides opportunity for the CDA candidate to reflect upon her training, her experience, and feedback from others about her work with young children. Instead of just being a means toward an end, a credential, the CDA process itself has become a valuable professional development experience. In a way, it has become more developmentally appropriate for early childhood professionals—valuing process over product!

This credentialing process has also shifted more responsibility to the candidate, who will need to meet specific deadlines, locate a Professional Development Specialist (called the PD Specialist), and schedule her own verification visit and CDA Exam. By allowing the candidate to take charge of her own CDA, the Council is encouraging her to be a responsible and goal-directed professional.

How Many People Have a CDA Credential?

Since 1975, the total number of caregivers who have achieved a CDA Credential is well over 300,000. As a result of an increased demand for trained and qualified staff by employers in both the public and private sectors, more than 15,000 child care providers apply for the CDA Credential each year. In addition, forty-nine states plus the District of Columbia include the CDA Credential as part of their child care licensing regulations (Bailey 2004).

Who Earns a CDA?

More than half of CDAs are between the ages of twenty-six and forty, with a continued increase in the number of CDAs over the age of forty. The majority of people who have earned a CDA are female. Those who are CDAs tend to be more diverse with regard to race/ethnicity (Bailey 2004).

Why Is Getting a CDA Important?

Working through the CDA process can be worthwhile and rewarding. In so doing, a candidate can benefit through these achievements:

- Earn a nationally recognized Credential
- Evaluate his or her own work as it compares to national standards and improve on skills
- Receive one-on-one advice, support, and feedback from early childhood professionals who have experience working with young children and knowledge of child development
- Improve upon existing skills to the benefit of young children, as well as the candidate

(Council for Professional Recognition 2006)

The field of early childhood education is a vibrant one, showing much potential for increased employment opportunity in the future. The National Occupational Outlook Handbook indicates that employment for child care workers is expected to grow by at least 20 percent by 2020, which is a faster average employment increase than that of any other occupation. With continued research indicating the critical importance of the first years in a child's life, the demand for quality child care is also increasing (Bureau of Labor Statistics 2012–13). Earning a CDA can put you into a good position for a promising career as a trained, early childhood professional.

Who Can Apply for a CDA?

Early childhood care and education workers who are in center-based, family child care, or home visitor programs can be evaluated by the Council. These persons need to have some education and experience in early child care and meet several requirements, specifically, these:

- Be eighteen years of age or older
- Hold a high school diploma or GED
- Be a high school junior or senior enrolled in a high school career/technical program in early childhood education
- Have 480 hours of experience working with young children in the same age group and setting as the CDA application
- Have 120 clock hours of formal child care education

(Council for Professional Recognition 2013)

What Kind of Formal Child Care Education Is Needed?

The 120 clock hours of formal child care education must include at least ten hours in each of the following subject areas:

- Planning a safe, healthy environment (safety, first-aid, health, nutrition, space planning, materials and equipment, play)
- Steps to enhance children's physical and intellectual development (large- and small-muscle development, language, discovery, art, music)
- Positive ways to support children's social and emotional development (self-esteem, independence, self-control, socialization)
- Strategies to establish productive relationships with families (parent involvement, home visits, conferences, referrals)
- Strategies to manage an effective program operation (planning, record keeping, reporting)
- Maintaining a commitment to professionalism (advocacy, ethical practices, work force issues, professional associations)

- Observing and recording children's behavior (tools and strategies for objective information collection)
- Principles of child growth and development (developmental milestones from birth to age five, cultural influences on development)

The training can be for college credit or for no credit. Formal courses that cover the previously mentioned topics might have titles such as these:

- Child Growth and Development
- Health, Safety, and Nutrition in Early Childhood Programs
- Guidance Techniques for Early Childhood
- Introduction to the Early Childhood Education Profession
- Emerging Literacy in Young Children
- Early Childhood Curriculum

You may need to look at the catalog description for a specific course to see what topics it covers. These hours of training must be obtained from an organization or agency that has expertise in training early childhood teachers:

- Four-year colleges and universities
- Two-year junior and community colleges
- Technical and vocational schools
- Early childhood education or child care programs that provide training, such as Family Services, school districts, Head Start, or employer-sponsored in-service training
- Programs offered by the state or federal government or by branches of the US Military Services

Please note that training obtained at conferences or from individual consultants is not accepted by the Council. A candidate may acquire the 120 clock hours of training from one single training program or from a combination of programs. Most CDAs receive their training through credit courses or continuing education units (CEUs). The Council provides a National Directory of Early Childhood Preparation Institutions listed by state on its website (www.cdacouncil.org) (Council for Professional Recognition 2006).

Although there is no longer any time restriction on the training, it is recommended that the training be taken no more than three years before beginning the CDA process. Research in the field of early childhood is advancing every day, and we in this profession need to stay current to provide the best care and education for young children.

Is Financial Assistance Available to Help Pay for My Training?

Some state and local organizations offer financial assistance for training as well as for the CDA assessment fees. For example, twenty-three states currently participate in a Teacher Education and Compensation Helps (T.E.A.C.H.) program. This program, which originated in North Carolina, gives scholarships to child care workers to complete coursework in early childhood education and to increase their compensation. To learn more about this program and to see a listing of participating states, you can visit the Child Care Services Association website (www.childcareservices.org/ps/teach.html). The Council for Professional Recognition has a link on its website for CDA Scholarship Funding, which provides information state by state (www.cdacouncil.org/resource-center/cda-scholarships). You will also want to inquire through your employer or local early childhood professional association for more information about financial assistance. You may also be able to find free or low-cost training through your local resource and referral agency (Council for Professional Recognition 2006).

Do I Have to Provide Some Kind of Proof That I Had This Training?

Each agency or organization providing the training must provide proof of the candidate's education by means of a letter, certificate, or transcript. The candidate will break down the 120 hours into the required subject areas on the Summary of My CDA Education sheet in the Professional Portfolio.

Are There Different Types of CDA Endorsements?

A candidate may choose from several different CDA endorsements, each in a different setting:
- Center-based infant/toddler
- Center-based preschool
- Family child care
- Home visitor

- Bilingual
- Special education

This choice depends on the candidate's specific experience with young children in whichever of the categories the candidate is working and where she can be observed functioning as a lead teacher. The candidate may not choose a setting in which she hopes or intends to work in the future. For example, if a candidate is working with infants and toddlers in a center-based program, she may not apply for a center-based preschool credential because she plans to move into a classroom of older children in the near future. She must first acquire a center-based infant/toddler credential because this is the setting in which she presently works and where she will be observed for her CDA. She may, at a later date, work toward a CDA for center-based preschool when she has accumulated 480 hours of experience with children in that age group and completes the credentialing process for that setting. All of the steps must be completed again for this new setting, but some of the training taken for the first CDA may be reused if it covers areas that relate to the second credential type. For example, a course that covered health and safety in child care could be counted toward the second credential, but a course specifically about infants could not be used for a preschool credential (Council for Professional Recognition 2006, 2013).

Once you have begun the CDA process and until your verification visit is completed, it is very important that you stay in the particular setting you have chosen. This is because all of your documentation, your CDA Exam, Family Questionnaires, and reflective dialogue with the PD Specialist will be based on that setting. Changing settings will not work. It may be necessary to explain this to your director so such changes are postponed until after this time. If you are a "floater" in a center, working with several different age groups and settings as needed, you must ask your director to let you settle into one specific setting and age group for the majority of the time while you are working on your CDA. Within three years of applying as a candidate, you must have 480 hours of experience working with children whose ages and setting are the same as those chosen for your application.

When you receive *The Child Development Associate National Credentialing Program® and CDA Competency Standards* book from the Council, it will be one of three different colors, depending on the specific setting (Family Child Care is blue, Center-Based Preschool is green, and Center-Based Infant/Toddler is yellow). It

Center-based programs can include nursery schools, child care, Head Start, lab schools, child development programs, or parent cooperatives. They can be full-time or part-time operations and have structured or unstructured schedules. These programs can be in universities, public schools, churches, or privately owned and operated. Programs that meet the CDA requirements for a center-based setting can be non-profit or for-profit.

Contact the Council (800–424–4310, www.cdacouncil.org) for more information on the home visitor setting, bilingual setting, or special education setting.

will have information about the CDA application requirements and process, with the entire midsection devoted to a thorough overview of the six Competency Standards. The back of each *Competency Standards* book includes a section of perforated documents, including an application form, cover sheets needed for the Professional Portfolio, the Comprehensive Scoring Instrument, and other documents that the you and the PD Specialist will use during the verification visit.

What Do These Settings Look Like?

CENTER-BASED PRESCHOOL SETTING This is a state-licensed child development center where a candidate is working with a group of at least eight children. All of the children in the group are ages three to five years. Also, the entire center-based program needs to have at least ten children enrolled with at least two caregivers working in the center with the children on a regular basis.

CENTER-BASED INFANT/TODDLER SETTING This is a licensed child development center at which a candidate can be observed working as a primary caregiver with a group of at least three children ages birth through thirty-six months. Also, the entire center-based program needs to have at least ten children enrolled with at least two caregivers working in the center with the children on a regular basis. Note that center-based programs can include nursery schools, day care, Head Start, lab schools, child development programs, or parent cooperatives. They can be full-time or part-time operations and have structured or unstructured schedules. These programs can be in universities, public schools, churches, or privately owned and operated. Programs that meet the CDA requirements for a center-based setting can be nonprofit or for-profit (Council for Professional Recognition 2006, 2013).

FAMILY CHILD CARE SETTING This is a family child care home in which a candidate is working with at least two children, ages five years old or younger. These children are not to be related to the candidate by either blood or marriage. This child care home must meet minimum state and local regulations, unless it is located where there is no regulation of family child care.

HOME VISITOR SETTING This is a program of home visits to families with young children from birth to five years old. Its main focus is providing support and education to parents, helping them meet the needs of their growing children.

BILINGUAL SETTING This is a child development program with specific goals for supporting bilingual development in children. In this setting, two languages are consistently used and parent involvement is encouraged to attain the program's bilingual goals. In addition to meeting all of the other standard requirements for earning a CDA, candidates seeking this specialization will need to show evidence (through a course description or syllabus) of having had training in Principles of Dual Language Learning as part of the required 120 clock hours. This would be indicated under subject area 2: "Advancing children's physical and intellectual development." When distributing the Family Questionnaires, the candidate will ask the families to pay close attention in answering question 14, which is specific to bilingual programs.

There will also be differences in the Professional Portfolio for the bilingual candidate. For example, in the Resource Collection, the candidate will present resources in both languages that are used directly with families and children. These would include Resource Collection items RC I–3, RC II, RC III, and RC IV. For the Reflective Statements of Competence, the candidate will write three in English and three in the second language. The candidate will also need to include information in all six of the Reflective Statements about how principles of dual-language learning are applied in daily practice with children. The Professional Philosophy Statement may be written in either language.

The PD Specialist (the person who will conduct the verification visit) chosen by the candidate must be proficient in both languages and have had direct experience in bilingual early childhood programs and with groups that are non–English speaking. The PD Specialist will conduct the reflective dialogue during the verification visit in both languages. The observation must take place in an early childhood program where both languages are used consistently every day. The candidate will demonstrate her use of the two languages during the observation. The Competency Standards outlined in the Council's *Competency Standards* books have several specific dual-language indicators flagged, which the PD Specialist will be looking for during the observation. The CDA Exam may be taken in either English or Spanish. If the candidate speaks a language other than Spanish, the exam will be taken in English. During the reflective dialogue, the PD Specialist will speak with the candidate in both languages.

MONOLINGUAL SETTING In this child development program, daily and consistent use of a language other than English is used. In most cases, this second language is Spanish. However, if the candidate speaks a language other than Spanish, he or she will need to contact the Council to make special arrangements for locating an eligible PD Specialist who speaks that language and for special accommodations for taking the CDA Exam. There will probably be an additional fee for these accommodations.

Besides meeting all of the other standard requirements for earning a CDA, the monolingual candidate will ask the families to complete the Family Questionnaires in either Spanish or English. In the Professional Portfolio, the Resource Collection items RC I–3, RC II, RC III, and RC IV, all of the Competency Statements, and the Professional Philosophy Statement, must be completed in Spanish.

The PD Specialist chosen by the candidate will be proficient in Spanish and will observe the candidate working with families and children who speak Spanish as the predominant language. The candidate will speak Spanish during the observation. The CDA Exam may be taken in either English or Spanish. During the reflective dialogue, the PD Specialist will converse with the candidate in Spanish.

SPECIAL EDUCATION SETTING This child development setting serves children who have moderate to severe special needs. Setting criteria will be the same as for center-based preschool, center-based infant/toddler, or family child care, based on the children's ages and the type of program.

In any of the settings mentioned already, a candidate may either be employed or working as a volunteer (Council for Professional Recognition 2006, 2013).

The CDA Process

The CDA process includes five stages: prepare, apply, demonstrate, earn, renew. Several parts of this process are completed even before you submit your application to the Council. These are the five stages:

1. Prepare

Any time before applying, the candidate must have the required education (have a high school diploma or GED or be in high school enrolled in an early childhood career/tech early childhood program) and have completed the required 120 clock hours of training, including ten hours in each of the CDA subject areas.

The candidate must choose one of the CDA settings, based on the children with whom she is working (center-based preschool, center-based infant/toddler, or family child care) and order the appropriate *Competency Standards* book from the Council for Professional Recognition. You will specify one of these settings when ordering. Ordering can be done by calling 1-800-424-4310 or by going online at www.cdacouncil.org.

The CDA candidate is assessed on the basis of six national CDA Competency Standards. The six standards are the criteria used to evaluate a caregiver's performance with children and families. These same six standards are used for all of the settings.

These are the six CDA Competency Standards:

I. To establish and maintain a safe, healthy learning environment

II. To advance physical and intellectual competence

III. To support social and emotional development and to provide positive guidance

VI. To establish positive and productive relationships with families

V. To ensure a well-run, purposeful program responsive to participant needs

VI. To maintain a commitment to professionalism

(Council for Professional Recognition 2006, 2013)

The six Competency Standards are defined in greater detail by thirteen Functional Areas. These Functional Areas describe more specifically the functions that a caregiver must perform to meet the criteria of each Competency Standard. These functions will vary according to a candidate's particular child care setting and the age groupings of the children.

Within six months of your application, you will distribute and collect Family Questionnaires. You will also assemble your Professional Portfolio, including the Resource Collection, six Competency Statements, and your Professional Philosophy Statement.

As a candidate, you will prepare a Professional Portfolio. The portfolio will include various pieces of documentation, a Resource Collection, six Competency Statements (based on the CDA Competency Standards), and a Professional Philosophy Statement. Specific instructions for assembling and preparing this portfolio are included in chapter 4 for a preschool setting, chapter 5 for an infant/toddler setting, and chapter 6 for a family child care setting.

Also prior to applying for a CDA, you will need to locate a PD Specialist. This is a person who has been trained and certified by the Council to conduct CDA verification visits. Read more about the PD Specialist later in this chapter.

One of the final steps in the CDA process will be to compose a Professional Philosophy Statement. It will be typed and placed into the last section of your portfolio. You will not write this Professional Philosophy Statement until you have completed these steps:

- Completed all of your CDA training
- Had at least 480 hours of experience working with young children
- Completely finished the Professional Portfolio

All of these combined experiences will enable you to write a fuller, more thoughtful, informed Professional Philosophy Statement.

To prepare for writing this philosophy statement, however, it is a good idea to think about how you feel about certain aspects of early childhood practices, based on your experience and training. This will help you to organize your thoughts. This may be the first time you have ever thought about your own personal philosophy of teaching young children, or if you have, you may not ever have written it down.

In appendix F is a Professional Philosophy Exercise, which involves a series of statements you will complete to prompt you to think about your beliefs and feelings. When asked, the majority of CDA candidates who have gone through this exercise before trying to write their philosophy statements said it was very valuable to them and made this task much easier. Rather than just a couple words, try to write a short paragraph as your response to each item, thinking deeply about what you're writing.

Right now, as you begin your CDA journey, take a few minutes to complete this exercise. You will be reviewing and using your responses later when you write the Professional Philosophy Statement. When you are finished, come back to this page and continue reading about the next stages of the CDA process.

2. Apply

Application can be done online on the Council's website (www. cdacouncil.org/yourcda) or by using the paper application form located at the back of your *Competency Standards* book. Your application fee accompanies the form. When the application has been accepted, the candidate will receive a Ready to Schedule Notice e-mail from the Council. At that time, you will schedule the CDA Exam and call the PD Specialist to schedule your verification visit.

3. Demonstrate

The CDA Exam and the verification visit can be scheduled in any order the candidate wishes. The CDA Exam is taken on a computer at a Pearson VUE Testing Center and consists of multiple-choice questions geared to the candidate's particular CDA setting. The verification visit consists of three parts:

1. **Review:** The PD Specialist will look over the candidate's documentation, including the Professional Portfolio.

2. **Observe:** The PD Specialist will observe the candidate working in her setting with young children for a two-hour period.

3. **Reflect:** The candidate will have a reflective dialogue with the PD Specialist about her professional strengths and areas that can be improved, along with setting some goals for professional development.

The first two parts of the verification visit—review and observe—are scored using the Comprehensive Scoring Instrument that is at the back of the *Competency Standards* book.

You will need to have your Professional Portfolio completed before the verification visit.

4. Earn

The PD Specialist submits scores for the observation and the verification visit within forty-eight hours of completion. These scores, along with the score for the CDA Exam, are combined for a cumulative score to determine the decision for credentialing. If this score meets the Council's requirement, the CDA Credential will be awarded and mailed to the candidate. If not, the candidate will be notified and provided with information about appeal procedures and other options.

5. Renew

The CDA Credential must be renewed every three years. Several pieces of documentation, along with a fee, are submitted along with the Renewal Application.

(Council for Professional Recognition, 2013)

The Professional Development Specialist

The PD Specialist must meet the requirements listed in the *Competency Standards* book:

• Have Internet access

• Possess a working e-mail address

- Be comfortable working with people of varied racial, ethnic, and socio-economic backgrounds
- Know local, state, and national standards and requirements for child care programs that serve children from birth to five years
- Conduct verification visits during early childhood programs' usual operating hours
- Be bilingual, if conducting a bilingual verification visit
- Speak the language of the Monolingual Specialization, if conducting a monolingual verification visit
- Have earned an associate's or bachelor's degree from an accredited university or college in one of these disciplines:
    - Early childhood education/child development
    - Elementary education/early childhood education
    - Home economics/child development
- Have studied, within the degree held, a minimum of eighteen credit hours or twenty-four quarter hours of coursework in early childhood education/child development, specific to children from birth to five years old
- Possess sufficient experience to meet one of these two requirement options:
    - Option 1. Those who hold a bachelor's degree or higher need at least two years working in a child care setting serving children from birth to five years old, with one year spent working directly with children as a caregiver, teacher, social worker, or similar role, and one year supporting the professional growth of at least one other adult.
    - Option 2. Those who hold an associate's degree need at least four years working in a child care setting with children from birth to five years old, with at least two years working directly with children as a caregiver, teacher, social worker, or similar role, and two years supporting the professional growth of at least one other adult.

The PD Specialist can be chosen from among people you know who have received this certification in your area or from among those listed in the Council's PD Specialist Directory. You can access the PD Specialist Directory on the Council's website at www.yourcda.org/Find-a-PDS/pds_search.cfm.

You will call a person listed in your area and get his or her identification number, which you will enter on your application form (Council for Professional Recognition 2013).

If you are choosing a PD Specialist from among people you know, it is important to consider whether any ethical conflicts of interest related to your particular relationship may interfere or even disqualify the person from serving as a PD Specialist for you. Here are some restrictions the Council has set forth about conflicts of interest:

A person may not, under any circumstances, serve as your PD Specialist if the person fits these descriptions:

- An immediate relative, such as your mother, father, sibling, spouse, son, or daughter
- Someone who is currently your direct supervisor
- A co-worker who teaches in the same group or classroom where you work

The Council also has a listing of other circumstances that warrant careful thought, as they may also be considered conflicts of interest:

- Someone who is your indirect supervisor
- A trainer, either direct or indirect
- Any person or representative of an organization that has financial or contractual considerations related to you or who may benefit in some way from your credentialing outcome
- Your employer
- A co-worker employed in the same facility, but not in your group or classroom
- Someone who is your peer or friend
- Any person who may hold a personal or professional bias toward or against you or any group to which you belong
- A licensing agent

The decision to choose an individual who fits one of these categories is up to you and the particular PD Specialist. As you begin to work together, you will both sign a Statement of Ethics (Council for Professional Recognition 2013).

As you can see, this process involves multiple steps. You should not have to go through this credentialing process alone. Even if you are the first teacher in your program to do this, someone should be supporting you and offering help. Perhaps you know another CDA candidate or someone who has already gone through the process. Or the instructor who provided your training hours might agree to mentor you. If you work in a child care center, your director can be a source of support. Chapter 2 is devoted to center directors and how they can help ensure the success of their teachers who are working on a CDA Credential. It would be a good idea to encourage your director to read it, so you might benefit from the added support only a director can provide.

A Word to Center-Based Program Directors: Supporting Your CDA Candidates

If you are a center director, you are faced with making sure your staff members acquire the training and qualifications they need to meet licensing requirements and to provide the best possible care for the children in your program. In light of recent research indicating the importance of the first five years of life in terms of children's optimal development, the Child Development Associate (CDA) Credential has become the basic, required qualification for lead child care providers in most states.

Quality child care depends on qualified, trained staff—period. Whether *you* have requested your teachers to get their CDAs or they have taken the honorable initiative to improve *themselves* through this process, the bottom line is the same: increased quality for your center. To be successful in earning a CDA Credential, your teachers will not only need to work hard to prepare themselves for the process, but they will also need an appropriate setting in which they can be observed by their CDA Professional Development (PD) Specialist.

As the director of the center, you play a very important role. You can be a source of support and help to your CDA candidate. In a sense, when a teacher is working toward a Credential, the entire program is too. If you have asked that your teachers get a CDA, your responsibility doesn't end there. They will not be going through this process as separate entities but will be using your center as the setting for their formal observation. If the setting does not meet the standards required by the Council for Professional Recognition (the agency that awards the CDA Credential), your teachers will have a difficult time earning a CDA.

Working toward a CDA Credential requires a good deal of effort on the part of the candidate, including 120 clock hours of formal early childhood training, assembling a comprehensive Professional Portfolio, and writing six Reflective Statements of Competence, each of which are about 500 words in length. Can you imagine the disappointment and frustration a teacher would experience if she had come this far, completed all the required training and documentation, and then realized the center where the formal observation was to take place wouldn't work—or worse yet, the director was not willing to do what it took to *make* it work?

Answers to Questions That Center Directors Frequently Ask

The following are some common questions asked by center directors, along with answers that may help you better understand the task ahead for your candidate.

1. *Who will come to my center?*

The person who will come to your center will be the candidate's Professional Development Specialist. The PD Specialist is acting as a representative of the Council for Professional Recognition in Washington, D.C. The PD Specialist's job is to assess the candidate's work with young children in a qualified early childhood setting and to report back to the Council.

The PD Specialist is a qualified, early childhood professional from the local area who has completed specialized training and been certified by the Council for Professional Recognition. The candidate was able to choose her own PD Specialist from among those she knew or those listed in the Council's online PD Specialist Directory.

The PD Specialist will spend about two hours observing your teacher, using a Comprehensive Scoring Instrument with indicators based on national CDA Standards. After the observation, the PD Specialist will meet with your teacher for about one-and-a-half hours to review her documentation and to conduct a reflective dialogue, which is a final, required part of the credentialing process. Ideally this will occur immediately following the observation, so if your building has a quiet, private room that can be used for this purpose, you can offer to let them use it. If this happens, you will need to make arrangements for someone to cover your teacher's room while she has this meeting.

2. What will the PD Specialist be looking for at my center?

For your teacher to demonstrate her knowledge and expertise in working with young children, she will need a classroom with appropriate equipment, materials, health and safety features, and operating procedures.

If one of your teachers is working on a CDA Credential, she probably has sent for and received a *Competency Standards* book. The book will either be yellow for infant/toddler or green for preschool settings. Ask to borrow the book so you can familiarize yourself with the Council's criteria for the appropriate setting, particularly part 2. If additional members of your staff will be earning the CDA Credential, you might consider purchasing a copy of each of these books for your own information. You can order them from the Council's website (www.cdacouncil.org).

3. What if something isn't the way it should be?

Prior to the CDA verification visit, your teacher will be completing a self-study, using the same Comprehensive Scoring Instrument as the PD Specialist will. If your teacher has indicated a problem area in her classroom, do your best to remedy the situation. Usually it is something minor and easily fixed. If you need clarification on exactly what is required, ask to see the Comprehensive Scoring Instrument.

4. If this is a licensed center, I have nothing to worry about, right?

Wrong! State licensing is a minimum operating standard for child care facilities. It does little to address developmentally appropriate practice and what is considered "quality" in an early childhood program. Read part 2 in the *Competency Standards* book for a clearer understanding of what the Council expects.

5. Do the families in my program play any part in this process?

Yes. The families' opinions of a candidate's work with their children are a very important part of assessing competency. This feedback will be used by your teacher to reflect on her practices, set goals, and make improvements. She will distribute Family Questionnaires provided by the Council to the families of the children she teaches. A majority (more than half) of these questionnaires need to be returned to her, so it might be helpful to encourage the families to return them in a timely fashion.

6. Some of my other teachers, who are not working on their CDA Credential, feel a little nervous and threatened by my teacher who is. Is this normal, and how should I handle it?

This happens, especially with teachers who have been at the center for many years. They may feel threatened by a coworker who is working to gain additional child care training and who is learning new and better ways of working with young children. These teachers may be afraid they will have to make abrupt changes in their usual way of doing things, or they may even fear losing their jobs to other teachers who are better trained. Some teachers don't care to be told to do things differently than they have been doing for many years, especially by a younger teacher with new ideas. At other times, staff members may be unclear or have false information about what a CDA Credential is and what is required to earn one.

It is in the center's best interest to put these misunderstandings and fears to rest. At a staff meeting, explain the CDA process or have someone come in to speak to the staff and hand out informational materials. Explain your center's policy of teamwork and support, and encourage the rest of the staff members to consider becoming CDAs, as well.

Above all, do *not* allow other staff members to treat your CDA candidate unfairly or with disrespect. Let the other teachers know that you value what this teacher is doing, that she has your full support, and that they should do likewise.

7. Should a center director consider becoming a CDA?

Absolutely! Unless you have an early childhood education degree, becoming a CDA would be a crucial part of any director's credentials and may even be required in your state. In any event, what an excellent example you would set for every member of your staff!

If you already have a CDA or a degree, you might consider becoming a PD Specialist. As the direct supervisor of your staff, you would not, of course, be able to conduct their verification visits due to conflict of interest. However, by going through the online training and certification process, you would have a better understanding of the CDA process and how you can best support your teachers. Also, you can conduct these verification visits for others outside of your program and earn $100 for each candidate you evaluate.

8. I'm ready to help my teachers. Where do I begin?

You can begin reviewing the six CDA Competency Standards and thirteen Functional Areas in part 2 of the *Competency Standards* book. Since the Competency Standards reflect developmentally appropriate practice and are aligned with the standards of the National Association for the Education of Young Children (NAEYC), following these standards will enhance the quality of your program as a whole. And if you plan to seek NAEYC accreditation in the future, complying with the Competency Standards is definitely a step in the right direction!

Here are some important items to be aware of:

FUNCTIONAL AREA 1: SAFE

- The facility should be generally safe and free from hazards. The furniture should be in good repair, with no broken toys or other materials.

- Electrical cords should not be within the children's reach. For example, when a CD or mp3 player is plugged in, is the cord exposed?

- When an outlet is not being used, it should have plastic safety caps inserted.

- A first-aid kit should be available in every classroom with basic supplies. If the kit is inside a cabinet, the cabinet door should be labeled to indicate where the kit is located.

- Emergency procedures (escape route, choking, Universal Precautions, basic first-aid, CPR, etc.) should be posted in the room.

- A listing or file of emergency contact numbers for the children should be located for easy access in the room.

- A listing should be available of persons authorized to pick up the children from your center.

- Area rugs should be secured to the floor.

- The outdoor playground should be safe. An adequate amount of some type of cushioning material needs to be in place under climbers, slides, and swings. Rusted or otherwise damaged equipment needs to be removed.

- Miniblind cords should be wound up and out of reach.

FUNCTIONAL AREA 2: HEALTHY

- Floors and carpeting should be clean.

- Covers on cots and crib sheets need to be washed at least weekly. They need to be clean at all times.

- Cots should be sanitized often, and children's bedding materials are kept separate.

- Toys and surfaces should be washed and sanitized daily.
- Health and immunization records should be kept up to date for each child.
- The facility should smell clean. There should be no unpleasant odors.
- Covered, plastic-lined trash cans should be available in the room.
- Restrooms should be clean.
- Warm water, liquid soap, and paper towels should be available for the children to use.
- The focus of snacks and meals should be good nutrition. No processed foods or junk foods should be served.
- Milk, water, or 100-percent fruit juices should be the only acceptable beverage choices.

FUNCTIONAL AREA 3: LEARNING ENVIRONMENT

- Books, toys, and other materials should be appropriate to the developmental level of the children.
- Books and materials should reflect cultural diversity and antibias (multicultural dolls, posters showing children of various ethnic and racial groups, no sexist or stereotypical items).
- Children's toys and materials should be stored on low, open shelves in easily accessible containers or bins that encourage independent use and clean up.
- A step stool should be provided at the sink, if necessary, so children can wash their hands by themselves.
- Child-sized furniture (tables and chairs) should be available.
- An ample variety of toys and materials, as well as duplicates of many toys, should be available.
- The room should be set up in activity centers so the children (including toddlers) can have opportunities to make choices during free-choice time. Here are some examples of centers you can offer:
  - Housekeeping area
  - Blocks
  - Art
  - Water table
  - Sand table

- Book corner
- Manipulatives
- Easel

- Children should not all be doing the same activity at the same time. For example, the whole group of toddlers should not sit down at a table for art. Art and other activities should be offered as choices during free-choice time.

- Circle time for young children should be very short and should consist of songs, fingerplays, short stories, movement activities, and the like. There should be no flash cards or drills.

FUNCTIONAL AREA 4: PHYSICAL

- Infants should be given ample "tummy time" on a clean floor surface, so they can explore and strengthen their upper bodies.

- Infants should spend only *short* periods of time in infant seats, bouncers, or swings.

- Children should have a daily opportunity for large-motor activities, indoors and out.

- Infants and toddlers should be offered a wide variety of interesting toys that are appropriate and safe.

FUNCTIONAL AREA 5: COGNITIVE

- Large blocks of guided free play time should be offered.

- Lots of interaction should occur between the children and caregivers. Caregivers should play with the children at every opportunity.

- Emphasis should be on children learning through play, with hands-on experiences.

- Available activities should provide opportunities for problem solving.

FUNCTIONAL AREA 6: COMMUNICATION

- A constant flow of communication should take place with the children, one-on-one, at their eye level.

- Caregivers should be good language models for the children.

- An ample number of quality children's books should be available.

FUNCTIONAL AREA 7: CREATIVE

- Provide unstructured play materials, such as blocks, paint, playdough, and musical instruments.
- Provide "messy" activities for children, such as fingerpainting, water and sand play, and watercolor markers.
- Allow toddlers to participate in creative art activities and with many of the same unstructured play materials as preschoolers, on a limited basis.
- Art activities should emphasize the process rather than a finished product of some kind.

FUNCTIONAL AREA 8: SELF

- Allow children to make choices in their activities.
- Provide one-on-one attention whenever possible.
- Respond quickly to an infant's distress.
- Hold and cuddle infants as much as possible.
- Give hugs and affection to toddlers and preschoolers.
- Display photos of the children and their families in the room at the children's eye level.

FUNCTIONAL AREA 9: SOCIAL

- Provide duplicates of popular toys.
- Provide consistent caregivers for infants and young children to promote attachment and bonding.
- Show positive social role models by care providers treating each other with respect.

FUNCTIONAL AREA 10: GUIDANCE

- Use positive guidance methods such as redirection, listening, and reinforcement.
- Have realistic expectations of young children's interests, attention spans, physical needs, and social abilities.

FUNCTIONAL AREA 11: FAMILIES

- Display a family bulletin board with upcoming events, parenting tips, and child development information in every room.
- Communicate with families in several ways, including newsletters and periodic conferences with the teachers.
- Encourage families to visit the center and participate in activities.

FUNCTIONAL AREA 12: PROGRAM MANAGEMENT

- Maintain up-to-date health and immunization records on all children.

- Provide regularly scheduled staff meetings and in-service training opportunities.

- Provide proper training for staff and encourage professional development.

FUNCTIONAL AREA 13: PROFESSIONALISM

- The staff in the center enjoys working with young children.

- Staff members are continually seeking to improve themselves by attending training courses and conferences.

- Staff members join a professional organization, such as NAEYC.

- Staff members are committed to a policy of confidentiality with the families in the program.

Tips and Suggestions from Former CDA Candidates and CDA Professional Development Specialists

- Be flexible and support the needs of your teacher. For example, if your program routinely includes worksheets as part of the daily activities, allow your teacher to substitute some type of hands-on alternative (for example, sorting, grouping, and measuring with different types of dried beans rather than a worksheet about numbers one through ten). The Council does not consider worksheets to be developmentally appropriate practice for use in early childhood programs, so your teacher's CDA PD Specialist will not expect to see any.

- If your center routinely provides art in the form of crafts (children assembling precut, preplanned projects, for example, a paper-plate Santa), allow your teacher to do creative art with the children when the PD Specialist visits. Creative art is process- rather than product-oriented, allowing children free expression and creativity with no predetermined outcome (for example, a collage). Crafts are not considered developmentally appropriate practice by the Council, and your teacher's PD Specialist will not expect to see them being done.

- Don't put your teacher into another classroom or age group once she has begun the CDA process. She needs to be in the same room consistently until the verification visit so that the families are familiar enough with her to complete the CDA Family Questionnaires. Also, your teacher has sent for and received a *Competency Standards* book for a specific setting and is gearing all of her work around that format. All of her work would be invalid in a different setting with a different group of children. She would need to send for different materials at an additional cost, redo some of the Professional Portfolio, and rewrite all of the Competency Statements. Don't do this to your candidate!

- The candidate may need copies of some of the forms you use at your center for the Resource Collection she is required to assemble. Ask what is needed and how you can help.

- If your center has a file of community resources (names and phone numbers of state, local, or national agencies) that support families, share this with the candidate. Some of the information may be needed for her Resource Collection.

When your teacher finally receives her CDA Credential, offer your sincere congratulations and suggest that she frame the certificate and display it proudly in your center. It will serve as a constant reminder of her commitment to professional excellence and as tangible evidence of your center's commitment to providing the best possible care for young children.

The next chapters explain the steps the candidate will take, whether in a preschool, infant/toddler, or family child care setting, as she prepares to earn her CDA. These steps include organizing the Professional Portfolio binder, as well as distributing, collecting, and evaluating the Family Questionnaires.

Preparing for the CDA Process

Organizing the Professional Portfolio Binder

Your first task will be to assemble a Professional Portfolio. Putting together your Professional Portfolio can be relatively easy, if you get yourself organized. The Council doesn't really care *how* the file is put together, as long as it is complete and legible. For example, it can be bound in a notebook or contained inside folders in a file box. Either way, items can easily be added or deleted.

Many early childhood educators are comfortable using a computer and related peripherals, and for them, the Council's recent announcement that candidates can create electronic Professional Portfolios is good news.

Electronic portfolios (e-portfolios) are becoming more popular for many different uses. Many four-year colleges and even some two-year institutions require students to create online portfolios to showcase their coursework, representing their entire academic tenure. In addition, some early childhood programs are creating e-portfolios for each of the children enrolled, recording progress and development with uploaded documentation, such as photos and work samples.

For the CDA Professional e-Portfolio, candidates can locate or create the resource items and then upload them into designated folders online. When the Reflective Statements of Competence and Professional Philosophy Statement are written, they are similarly included.

This process eliminates printing materials on paper. Each section of the e-portfolio template is set up in sequence and will indicate to the user when it has been completed.

E-portfolios are a good choice for those who have some computer proficiency, know how to use a scanner, and understand how to save and upload files, photos, and attachments. Companies providing e-portfolios offer tech support to help. Of course, collecting and creating the portfolio contents are still the candidate's responsibility, and the companies provide no help with that.

Access to an e-portfolio program is through a paid yearly subscription, usually between $20 and $35 a year. A candidate can continue to access the completed e-portfolio online as long as the subscription is active. If the candidate chooses to end the subscription, the portfolio files will need to be downloaded as a PDF file and then kept in that format or printed off and put into a binder.

Even though a candidate can choose to create an electronic version of the CDA Professional Portfolio, the Council for Professional Recognition is still, of course, accepting the portfolio in the traditional binder format, as well. The Council realizes that not every candidate feels comfortable enough with technology and some candidates may prefer to put together a traditional binder. Also, some people really enjoy the hands-on assembly of a binder and the addition of their own personal touches. If the binder is set up and organized properly, the candidate can see at a glance which components have been completed and which still need to be finished.

I suggest a one-and-a-half- or two-inch loose-leaf (three-ring) binder. It is helpful to get one that has a clear plastic sleeve on the front, so you can slip in a cover sheet with the title "Professional Portfolio," your setting, and your name. The advantage of the three-ring binder over the file box is its portability. It is rather inconvenient to carry around a file box. Also, it is much easier to look through a binder because everything is bound inside, not sliding around in file folders. To make your portfolio attractive, well organized, and easy for the Professional Development Specialist (also called the PD Specialist) to evaluate, I will provide some specific suggestions for setting it up.

You will need to have the *Child Development Associate National Credentialing Program and CDA Competency Standards* book handy, which was purchased from the Council. It will be green, blue, or yellow, depending on your particular setting. Refer to this *Competency Standards* book as you read the following suggestions for compiling your Portfolio.

These are the supplies you will need for your binder:

- One-and-a-half-inch or two-inch three-ring view binder
- Set of eight dividers with tabs
- Forty-five clear page protectors

- One-by-four-inch self-adhesive labels
- One-half-inch by one-and-three-quarters-inch self-adhesive labels
- One letter-sized sheet of cardstock

You will first type the small labels that will go on the eight side tabs of the dividers:

B   Family Questionnaires

C   Competency Standard I

D   Competency Standard II

E   Competency Standard III

F   Competency Standard IV

G   Competency Standard V

H   Competency Standard VI

I   Professional Philosophy Statement

Note that you will be starting with B and not A. This is because you will be using a set of eight dividers, not nine, to accommodate all of the sections. Since section A, Summary of My CDA Education, is self-explanatory, there is really no need to provide a designated section for it, so you will begin with section B for the Family Questionnaires. This way, you will not need to purchase two sets of eight tab dividers and only use one tab of the second set.

Place the dividers into the binder. In front of all of the dividers, place three empty page protectors. Look in the back of your *Competency Standards* book. You will see a page titled "My CDA Professional Portfolio." Carefully tear out this page along the perforations and place it in the first page protector. Next, find the Summary of My CDA Education page. Tear out this page and put it into the second page protector. Now there is one empty page protector left. This will be used to store all of your CDA training certificates and/or transcripts.

Behind divider B, place two empty page protectors. In the back of the *Competency Standards* book, locate the Family Questionnaires Summary Sheet. Tear out this page and place it into the first empty page protector behind divider B. The next empty page protector is where you will store all of the Family Questionnaires after you have sent them out and collected them back.

Behind dividers C through H will be the Resource Collection items. You will be typing labels for the page protectors that hold them. Instructions for doing so and information about what should go into the page protectors will be provided in the next chapters, based on your particular setting.

Distributing and Collecting the Family Questionnaires

How families view the CDA candidate, in terms of knowledge and skill, is very important. Families who have a child in the candidate's classroom will fill out a Family Questionnaire. With other changes in the CDA process, there also have been changes in how the Family Questionnaires are used and evaluated. Candidates will now read the responses on these questionnaires, using this information to determine their strengths and any areas needing improvement from the families' viewpoints. The candidate will be the only person to read these questionnaires.

At the back of the *Competency Standards* book is a reproducible, two-page Family Questionnaire. Carefully pull out this sheet and make enough copies for every family in your program to receive one. On the first page, there is a place to write in your name. There is also a place to indicate when you would like the questionnaire returned to you. Do not insert a date more than three days out, because then you may never get them back.

The candidate will contact each family in person, by phone, or in a newsletter, explaining a little bit about the CDA Credential, why she is interested in earning one, and the importance of obtaining the Family Questionnaires from every family in her program, even though completing one is entirely optional. The candidate may also distribute these questionnaires at a group meeting, or they can be mailed out to families, along with a self-addressed, stamped envelope. Only one questionnaire will be filled out per family. The best way to ensure the most questionnaires being returned is to catch family members when they drop off or pick up their children and ask them to complete these on the spot. Explain that there are only fourteen items on the questionnaire, which will take only a few minutes to complete. It is required that the candidate collect a majority of the total number distributed, or more than half.

At the back of the *Competency Standards* book, behind the Family Questionnaire that was pulled out, is a Family Questionnaire Summary Sheet. This should now be in the first page protector in section B for your binder. Take it out and print your name at the top. You will get a candidate identification number when you submit your application to the Council, so you can leave it blank for now. There are spaces for recording how many questionnaires you distributed and how many you collected. Fill these in.

Reviewing the Family Questionnaires

Each item on the Family Questionnaire is rated with a 3, 2, or 1. A rating of 3 indicates "Very capable" and is an area of strength. A rating of 2 indicates "Capable/competent." A rating of 1 indicates "Needs improvement" and is an area for professional growth.

Sometime prior to the verification visit with the PD Specialist, you will read each of the Family Questionnaires you collected. As you look at the responses and perhaps some of the additional written feedback the families provided, determine a couple of the strengths they identified in your work with their children and with them. These would be the items they rated a 3. Now based on the responses and feedback, determine a couple of areas the families indicated as needing some improvement. These would be the items they rated a 1.

Go back to the Family Questionnaires Summary Sheet. On this sheet, you will write what the families identified as your strengths and areas for future professional growth (weaknesses) into the appropriate sections provided. Then if you turn to the next page in your *Competency Standards* book, you will find the CDA Verification Visit Reflective Dialogue Worksheet. At the bottom, in boxes A and B, copy this same information about your strengths and areas for future professional growth. Do not write anything into boxes C through F. These will be completed during the reflective dialogue with the PD Specialist at the verification visit. You will prepare for this in chapter 8.

The following chapters include step-by-step instructions for assembling your Professional Portfolio, writing the Competency Statements, and composing your Professional Philosophy Statement. You will find the help you need, specific to your age-level endorsement and setting, in chapter 4 for center-based preschool, chapter 5 for center-based infant/toddler, or chapter 6 for family child care.

The CDA Process: Center-Based Preschool

Your decision to teach preschool children is an important one. These early years are when children develop first friendships, develop a good sense of self-esteem, gain a basic understanding of the world around them, and learn to be independent. As their teacher, you are responsible for providing a developmentally appropriate environment and experiences that will form a strong foundation for their future development and success in school. This is not a responsibility to be taken lightly, because it is your skill and effectiveness in the classroom that ultimately determine the quality of the entire program.

To get a position in a quality child development center (or retain the position you already have), to expect advancement, and to demand proper compensation, you are pursuing a Child Development Associate (CDA) Credential and becoming an early childhood professional. As such, you will need to demonstrate your competency in meeting the needs of preschool children. Having completed the 120 clock hours of training, you are ready to begin the CDA process. Your Professional Portfolio should now be set up and ready to fill with the Resource Collection.

The Resource Collection

You should already have your Portfolio preliminarily set up, after following the instructions in chapter 3. Next, you will print some one-by-four-inch labels for the dividers to correspond with the small labels on the tabs.

The first divider tab should be labeled **B Family Questionnaires**. Type a one-by-four-inch label with the same information and place it in the center of this divider page. Dividers C through H are for the Competency Statements and Resource Collection items for each of the six Competency Standards.

You will type a one-by-four-inch label to place in the center of each of these tabbed dividers as follows:

C   Tab: **Competency Standard I**
     Label: *Reflective Competency Statement I*
            CS I Resource Collection

D   Tab: **Competency Standard II**
     Label: *Reflective Competency Statement II*
            CS II Resource Collection

E   Tab: **Competency Standard III**
     Label: *Reflective Competency Statement III*
            CS III Resource Collection

F   Tab: **Competency Standard IV**
     Label: *Reflective Competency Statement IV*
            CS IV Resource Collection

G   Tab: **Competency Standard V**
     Label: *Reflective Competency Statement V*
            CS V Resource Collection

H   Tab: **Competency Standard VI**
     Label: *Reflective Competency Statement VI*
            CS VI Resource Collection

The tab on the last divider is labeled **I Professional Philosophy Statement**. Make a one-by-four-inch label with the same information to place in the center of this divider.

Labeling the Page Protectors and Collecting the Resources

You will be using one-by-four-inch labels for the page protectors. Each label will be placed at the upper right corner of a page protector, so it does not obstruct the items placed inside.

Behind the Summary of My CDA Education cover sheet is an empty page protector. Make a label for it:

> **Training Certificates/Transcripts**

This is the page protector that will hold all of your training certificates and/or transcripts.

In section B, behind the Family Questionnaires Summary Sheet is an empty page protector. Make a label for it:

> **Family Questionnaires**

This is the page protector that will hold all of your collected Family Questionnaires.

Now you will be placing page protectors and making labels for each of the Resource Collection items. Some labels have more information to be typed on them than others. You will have to adjust the size of the type you use so that the information will fit on the label.

Begin with section **C Competency Standard I**.

Behind the divider, place four page protectors. For the first page protector, type this label:

> **Competency Statement I**

When you have written your Competency Statement I, it will be placed in this page protector. (Later in this chapter, we will discuss writing the Competency Statements.)

For the second page protector, type this label:

> **RC I–1**
> Proof of completion of a first-aid course
> and a pediatric CPR course.

Photocopies of your first-aid and CPR course certificates or cards of completion can be placed in the page protector, but you will need the original documents on the day of the verification visit. An online course for this training is not acceptable. Training must be from a nationally recognized organization, such as the American Red Cross or the American Heart Association. The certification must be for a *pediatric* CPR course and must be current the day of your verification visit. If it is the wrong type or expired, the CDA process will be stalled until this is corrected.

For the third page protector, type this label:

> ## RC I–2
> A menu for one week.

If you can, provide a menu that you have actually served to children in your program or have created yourself. If this is not possible, you may find an appropriate menu on the Internet. Place the menu in this page protector. Later, when you write your Competency Statement I, you will be reflecting on the menu you included here, discussing why you feel it is or is not appropriate for meeting the nutritional needs of young children.

For the fourth page protector, type this label:

> ## RC I–3
> A weekly plan of learning experiences.

You can use the weekly activity plan form you usually use in your program, perhaps enlarging it to accommodate the information that is required. Be sure to address all of the typical learning areas, such as art, language/literacy, circle, fine- and gross-motor skills, dramatic play, math, and science. In addition to listing the activities, you need to write the learning goals for each activity, what you expect the children to learn, or how their development will be enhanced by doing the activity. You will indicate the age group for which the plan is intended (three-, four-, or five-year-olds). You must also explain if or how each of your activities could be adapted to enable a child who has special needs to participate. This can be for an actual child you have in your program or a fictitious child.

At the top of the weekly plan, indicate the child by first initial and brief statement of the special need:

Children with Special Needs: M. has cerebral palsy.

Let's say one of your activities was a nature walk. Under that activity you would indicate the accommodation that M. would need in order to participate:

Accommodations: Needs aide to push her wheelchair.

If no accommodation is needed for a particular activity (listening to a story at circle time, for example), you would indicate this:

Accommodations: None required.

For an example of this, see the Sample Weekly Activity Plan for Preschoolers provided in appendix E. There you will also find a listing of websites that will help you design accommodations for children who have special needs.

You have now completed collecting resources for Competency Standard I and are ready to move to section **D Competency Standard II**. Behind the divider, place ten page protectors.

For the first page protector, type this label:

Competency Statement II

When you have written your Competency Statement II, place it in this page protector.

The first group of resources is a collection of activity plans. You will create nine different activities for preschoolers. Create three of the activities for three-year-olds, three for four-year-olds, and three for five-year-olds.

For the second page protector, type this label:

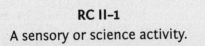

RC II–1
A sensory or science activity.

You will create a science or sensory activity. Examples might include a "feely bag" activity or a floating and sinking experiment.

It is best to use some type of simple activity plan template. On the form, you will indicate the type of activity. For this one, you would indicate "Science or Sensory Activity." You would also indicate for which age group it was intended (three-year-olds, four-year-olds, or five-year-olds), the goal(s) of the activity, the materials needed, the process or procedures, and teaching strategies. Then you will briefly discuss why the activity is developmentally appropriate for that particular age group. See a sample activity plan form provided in appendix C. There you will also find a listing of websites that will help you design accommodations for children with special needs.

For the third page protector, type this label:

> **RC II–2**
> An activity for language or literacy.

You will create a language or literacy activity. Examples might include reading a story with the children or playing a word game. You will designate for which age this activity is designed. Use the activity plan form.

For the fourth page protector, type this label:

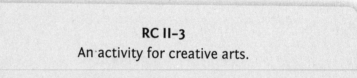

> **RC II–3**
> An activity for creative arts.

You will create a creative arts activity. Examples might include fingerpainting or making a collage. Be sure the activity you create is a "creative" one. You will not want to describe a craft activity that results in some type of product, but rather an activity in which the predominant emphasis is on the process. This will make it easy for you to explain why it is developmentally appropriate. You will designate for which age this activity is designed. Use the activity plan form.

For the fifth page protector, type this label:

> **RC II–4**
> An indoor fine-motor activity.

You will create an indoor fine-motor activity. Examples might include working with playdough or a cutting activity using scissors. You will designate for which age this activity is designed. Use the activity plan form.

For the sixth page protector, type this label:

> **RC II–5**
> An outdoor gross-motor activity.

Examples are provided solely for the purpose of demonstrating the types of activities that are expected. You need to create your own activities for these Resource Collection items, based on the particular group of children with whom you work.

You will create an outdoor gross-motor activity. Examples might include an obstacle course, rolling a ball into a target, or playing a game such as "Red Light, Green Light." You will designate for which age this activity is designed. Use the activity plan form.

For the seventh page protector, type this label:

> **RC II–6**
> An activity that supports children's self-concept.

You will create a self-concept activity. Examples might include drawing or painting self-portraits, sharing a favorite possession at circle time, or singing a song together with the children's names in it. You will designate for which age this activity is designed. Use the activity plan form.

For the eighth age protector, type this label:

> **RC II–7**
> An activity that supports children's
> emotional development or self-regulation.

You will create an emotional skills or self-regulation activity. Examples may include a simple table game that requires taking turns or a "Matching Faces" game using photos of people showing different emotions. You will designate for which age this activity is designed. Use the activity plan form.

For the ninth page protector, type this label:

> **RC II–8**
> An activity that supports children's
> development of social skills.

You will create a social skills activity. Examples might include a circle game or an activity that requires children to work in pairs or small groups. You will designate for which age this activity is designed. Use the activity plan form.

For the tenth page protector, type this label:

> **RC II–9**
> An activity for math.

You will create a math activity. Examples might include matching number cards or counting and sorting. You will designate for which age this activity is designed. Use the activity plan form.

Place the completed activity plan forms *into* the labeled page protectors.

You have now completed collecting resources for Competency Standard II and are ready to move to section **E Competency Standard III**. Behind the divider, place two page protectors.

For the first page protector, type:

> **Competency Statement III**

When you have written your Competency Statement III, place it in this page protector.

For the second page protector, type this label:

> **RC III**
> A bibliography of ten developmentally
> appropriate children's books.

Each book should be a different title and topic about things related to children's lives or situations that may challenge them. These can be books that help children deal with issues such as death, moving to a new home, starting a new school, or a new baby joining the family. These are known as *bibliotherapy* or *therapeutic* books. Or you may choose books about routines or activities children typically experience every day, such as making friends, going to school, or visiting grandparents. Do *not* cut and paste information from an Internet bookstore. These are to be books you have actually used with the children in your program and with which you are very familiar.

If your classroom book collection does not have many or any of these types of books, I would suggest going to the library and bringing back a wide selection that are age and developmentally appropriate for your particular group of children. Then read them to the children. After you do so, these books will qualify to be included in the Resource Collection, because then they are "books you have used with young children."

Type the information requested on one or two pages. Include each book's title, author, publisher, copyright date, and a short summary. Insert the pages back to back in this page protector.

You have now completed collecting resources for Competency Standard III and are ready to move to section **F Competency Standard IV**. Behind the divider, place seven page protectors.

For the first page protector, type this label:

Competency Statement IV

When you have written your Competency Statement IV, place it in this page protector.

The Resource Collection items for this section are a selection of helpful agencies and programs for families. These comprise the Family Resource Guide. The Council asks you to include four specific resources and suggests you locate several more resources in your particular community that would be helpful to families.

For the second page protector, type this label:

RC IV–1
Information for a local family-counseling agency.

Locate the address, phone number, and website address of the agency. Type the information you've found onto a sheet of paper and place it in this page protector.

For the third page protector, type this label:

RC IV–2
Information about an agency that provides translation services for English as a Second Language (ESL) and for American Sign Language.

This could be one service agency or two. Try to locate agencies in your community that would be easy for families to access. Type this information on a sheet of paper and place in this page protector.

For the fourth page protector, type this label:

> **RC IV-3**
> Information about two or more community agencies that provide resources and services for children who have special needs.

Find information about two or three agencies, which might include those that provide physical therapy, occupational therapy, speech therapy, or developmental or learning services. In some communities, the local school district provides these services. Be sure these are local agencies that families enrolled in your program can access. Include the agencies' names and contact information, along with a short description of the services they provide. Type this information and place it in this page protector.

For the fifth page protector, type this label:

> **RC IV-4**
> Three or more websites, and articles from each, that provide families with information about children's learning and development.

Type the information about each website, as requested. These websites could include those for NAEYC (www.naeyc.org), Zero to Three (www.zerotothree.org), Early Childhood News (www.earlychildhoodnews.org), or similar organizations. From each website, download and print one recent article. One of the articles you find and print must relate to child guidance. Place your typed information and the three articles into this page protector.

For the sixth, seventh, and eighth page protectors, type three of these labels, one for each protector:

> **Additional Helpful Family Resource**

Place these labels on the remaining three empty page protectors. Locate three more helpful resources in your community that would be useful to families. These might include your local agencies that provide food stamps, utility assistance, or child care vouchers. Type the name, description of services provided, and con-

Remember, you can add even more helpful resources, if you like. Just add more page protectors to hold them. Such a comprehensive collection of resources will be valuable to you when families are in need of assistance.

tact information for each agency you found on separate pieces of paper. Place these in the three page protectors labeled "Additional Helpful Family Resource," one page per protector.

You have now completed collecting resources for Competency Standard IV and are ready to move to section **G Competency Standard V**. Behind the divider, place three page protectors.

For the first page protector, type this label:

Competency Statement V

When you have written your Competency Statement V, place it in this page protector.

For the second page protector, type this label:

RC V
Three record-keeping forms, including
a blank accident report, a blank emergency form,
and a completed observation tool.

Locate a blank accident report form and a blank emergency form you use in your program. Then you will conduct an observation in your classroom. For the observation tool, you can use the Anecdotal Record Form provided in appendix B. Don't put the child's name on this form—just a first initial would be fine. The observation can be handwritten as long as it is legible. Place these three forms, back to back, in the three page protectors.

You have now completed collecting resources for Competency Standard V and are ready to move to section **H Competency Standard VI**. Behind the divider, place six page protectors.

For the first page protector, type this label:

Competency Statement VI

When you have written your Competency Statement VI, place it in this page protector.

For the second page protector, type this label:

> **RC VI–1**
> The name of and information about
> your state's child care regulatory agency.

Type the name of the agency, its address, and its phone number. You can find your state's child care regulatory agency by going to the National Resource Center for Health and Safety in Child Care and Education website: http://nrckids.org/STATES/states.htm.

Then click on your state, and you will find the state licensing contact. Click on the "Regulations" link for child care centers. There you will be able to view and print the sections describing staff, group size, and adult-child ratio requirements that you need to include.

Place the information you typed into this page protector and the sections you printed from the Regulations in the third empty page protector behind it.

For the fourth page protector, type this label:

> **RC VI–2**
> Information about two or three
> early childhood associations.

These associations may be national, state, regional, or local. They could include the National Association for the Education of Young Children (NAEYC, www.naeyc.org) or the National Association of Child Care Professionals (NACCP, www.naccp.org). Include the web address of each, as well as information about the available professional resources and how to become a member. Type the information and place it in this page protector.

For the fifth page protector, type this label:

> **RC VI–3**
> Your state's policies for reporting
> child abuse and neglect.

You can find the information about your particular state's policies by going to the Child Welfare Information Gateway (sponsored by the US Department of Health and Human Services) at www.childwelfare.gov/preventing/overview/state.cfm. You will notice that you need two pieces of information for this Resource Collection item:

1. Summary of the legal requirements for reporting child abuse and neglect

2. Contact information for the state child abuse/neglect agency in your state (web address, phone number/address)

Type this information and place it into this page protector.

This completes your Resource Collection! Go to the first page of your Professional Portfolio. On the My CDA Professional Portfolio cover sheet, check off item A, (having this cover sheet in your Portfolio). You will check off item B after you have collected all of your Family Questionnaires. Now go through items C through H, checking off the Resource Collection items for each. You will check off the Reflective Competency Statements for each of these items after they are written. Leave item I unchecked for now, until you write your Professional Philosophy Statement.

Writing the Reflective Statements of Competence

The national Competency Standards are used to evaluate a CDA candidate's skills in working with young children, families, their coworkers, and the community. There are six Competency Standards that define professional caregiver performance. Under each of the Competency Standards are one or more (thirteen in all) Functional Areas. The Functional Areas define more specifically the skills and behaviors the candidate must perform to meet each of the Competency Standards. You should read the six Competency Standards with the accompanying Functional Areas in part 2 of your *Competency Standards* book. This information also appears in a "Preschool Competency Standards At-A-Glance" chart in this section.

You will write six reflections based on your own teaching and interaction with young children, one reflection for each of the six CDA Competency Standards. Each statement will start with a discussion about how you meet each of the Functional Areas associated with it and then continue with a few other specific reflections, some of which will ask you to comment on items in the Resource Collection. Each statement, including all of its parts, should be no more than 500 words.

We will be looking in two sections of the *Competency Standards* book as you write your Competency Statements:

Part 1: "Earning the Child Development Associate (CDA) Credential" subsection "The Reflective Statements of Competence"

Part 2: "The Child Development Associate Competency Standards"

You will start Competency Statement I by creating a heading:

Competency Statement I
To establish and maintain a safe,
healthy learning environment

This will be typed in bold print, with the second line in italics.

In part 2 of your book, on the "At-A-Glance" chart, you will see that this Competency Standard has three Functional Areas: Safe, Healthy, and Learning Environment. Your initial paragraphs will describe how your teaching practices meet this standard in each of the Functional Areas.

Under the heading you created, write, in bold print, headings for the three Functional Areas, followed by your descriptions and examples. You can get some ideas by looking in part 2 of your *Competency Standards* book at the Indicators and Examples provided for Competency Standard I. However, you may not use these in your own statement. What you write must describe what happens in your particular program. Here are examples of what this might look like:

Functional Area 1: Safe
Safety is a main priority in the environment I provide for the children in my care. I make every effort to prevent injuries and accidents. For example, I check all play equipment before the children play on it. I also conduct fire drills once a month.

Functional Area 2: Healthy
In my program, I encourage and model healthy habits, such as hand washing and covering sneezes and coughs. I also sit at the table with the children at lunch to encourage them to eat the healthy foods they are served.

Functional Area 3: Learning Environment
I provide developmentally appropriate activities and materials for the children to learn through guided play. Learning materials are kept on low, open shelves, so the children can choose for themselves.

Looking back at part 1 of the *Competency Standards* book in the Reflective Statements of Competence section, you will see that this statement has three additional parts: CS I a, CS I b, and CS I c. Make a heading for each in bold print:

CS I a

Remember, these examples are provided only for clarification and should not be used as part of your own Competency Statements. The examples you write should reflect your particular program, practices, and group of children.

Write at least one paragraph reflecting on the sample menu you placed in your Resource Collection. If you designed the menu, stand behind it and justify your food choices based on your own knowledge and concern about the nutritional needs of children. If you were not the one who designed the menu but only served the meals, reflect on the strengths and weaknesses you see in the food choices. Discuss what you would change, if anything.

CS I b

Think about the room environment where you will be observed by the PD Specialist. Does this environment represent a place where children can learn best, according to your own philosophy? How? If you were not the one to set up this environment, discuss its strengths and weaknesses. If you had the opportunity, what would you change about it?

CS I c

Look at the weekly activity plan you chose for your Resource Collection. Does this plan align with your own philosophy of how children learn best? If you were not the one to create this weekly plan, discuss its strengths and weaknesses. If you had the opportunity, what would you change about it?

Now you have finished all the parts of Competency Statement I. Check the word count. If it is fewer than 500 words, add a few more examples for the Functional Areas. If it is more than 500 words, take something out. Print this document and place it in the first page protector behind divider C.

You are ready to go on to Competency Standard II. Start a new page and create a heading:

Competency Standard II
To advance physical and intellectual competence

In part 2 of your book, on the "At-A-Glance" chart, you will see that this Competency Standard has four Functional Areas: Physical, Cognitive, Communication, and Creative. Your initial paragraphs will describe how your teaching practices meet this standard in each of the Functional Areas.

Under the heading you created, write, in bold print, headings for the four Functional Areas:

Functional Area 4: Physical

Functional Area 5: Cognitive

Functional Area 6: Communication

Functional Area 7: Creative

Under each of these headings, you will describe how the Functional Area is met in your program, giving some examples. You can get some ideas by looking in part 2 of your *Competency Standards* book at the Indicators and Examples provided for Competency Standard II. However, you may not use these in your own statement. What you write must describe what happens in your particular program. Here are examples of what this might look like:

Functional Area 4: Physical

In my program, I provide opportunities for children to develop both small- and large-motor skills, and I model enjoyment and active participation in physical activity. On our playground, we have climbers and slides. Indoors, the children enjoy using scissors and playdough to develop their small muscles.

Functional Area 5: Cognitive

I make available materials and activities that enable children to explore, problem solve, ask questions, and follow their interests. I provide sorting and matching games, and I ask lots of open-ended questions as they play.

Functional Area 6: Communication

I encourage children to communicate with each other, with me, and with other adults in my program, as well as support their emerging literacy by offering a writing center and labeling the room. I also label items and areas in the room in both English and Spanish.

Functional Area 7: Creative

I give children opportunities to express their creativity. They experience more process art than assembling products. We have a dramatic play area with props that offer opportunities for make-believe and role play. We also have a puppet theater and box of puppets.

Looking back at part 1 of the *Competency Standards* book in the Reflective Statements of Competence section, you will see that this Statement has four additional parts: CS II a, CS II b, CS II c, and CS II d. Make a heading for each in bold print:

CS II a

Pick one of the nine learning activities you created for your Resource Collection (RC II). This activity should align with your philosophy of how to best support children's *physical* development. Explain how it does. You will want to choose either the indoor fine-motor activity or the outdoor gross-motor activity, because these support physical development and will be easy to discuss.

CS II b

Pick one of the nine learning activities you created for your Resource Collection (RC II). This activity should align with your philosophy of how to best support children's *cognitive* development. Explain how it does. You will want to choose your science/sensory or your mathematics activity, because these support cognitive development and will be easy to discuss.

CS II c

Pick a third learning experience you created for your Resource Collection (RC II). This activity should align with your philosophy of how to best support children's *creative* development. Explain how it does. You will want to choose your creative arts activity to discuss for this one.

CS II d

Write a paragraph describing how you promote *language* and *communication* development of all the children in your program, including those who are dual-language learners. For ideas, look in part 2 of the *Competency Standards* book, Competency Standard II (Functional Area 6: Communication). For examples specific to dual-language learners, look in part 3 of the *Competency Standards* book at Principles for Dual Language Learners.

Now you have finished all the parts of Competency Statement II. Check the word count, making sure it is right around 500 words. Print this document and place it in the first page protector behind divider D.

You are ready to go on to Competency Statement III. Start a new page and create a heading:

Competency Statement III
*To support social and emotional development
and to provide positive guidance*

In part 2 of your book, on the "At-A-Glance" chart, you will see that this Competency Standard has three Functional Areas: Self, Social, and Guidance. Your initial paragraphs will describe how your teaching practices meet this standard in each of the Functional Areas.

Under the heading you created, write, in bold print, headings for the three Functional Areas:

Functional Area 8: Self

Functional Area 9: Social

Functional Area 10: Guidance

Under each of these, you will describe how the Functional Area is met in your program, with some examples. You can get some ideas by looking in part 2 of your *Competency Standards* book at the Indicators and Examples provided for Competency Standard III. However, you may not use these in your own statement. What you write must describe what happens in your particular program. Here are examples of what this might look like:

Functional Area 8: Self

I provide opportunities for children to feel independent, successful, and good about themselves. They pack their own backpacks and help to pick up their own toys after playing. I offer encouragement and praise their efforts.

Functional Area 9: Social

I encourage children to get along with each other and to make friends. I make opportunities for sharing and cooperation through games and table activities, and I encourage them to help each other.

Functional Area 10: Guidance

I use developmentally appropriate strategies to help children learn acceptable behaviors and self-regulation, as well as assisting those who may have more challenging behaviors. I use redirection whenever possible and use time-out sparingly. We have a set of simple rules we wrote together, posted on the wall in words and pictures.

Looking back at part 1 of the *Competency Standards* book in the Reflective Statements of Competence section, you will see that this statement has two additional parts: CS III a and CS III b. Make a heading for each in bold print:

CS III a

Write a paragraph about how you support favorable *self-concepts* and *social-emotional skills* of the children in your program. You will provide specific examples of what you do with children in your program to support these skills. Examples might be providing children encouragement to try things on their own, allowing them to print their own names on their projects, or giving them opportunities to share something special from home at circle time.

You might also use examples such as providing opportunities for children to share materials and to play games together.

CS III b

Think about your philosophy of encouraging children's *positive* behaviors. Can you see similarities or differences between your philosophy and the kind of guidance you were given as a child? Then describe strategies you use to effectively handle children's *challenging* behaviors.

Note: You will see that there are three parts to this item. Write a paragraph for each part:

1. **Think about your philosophy of encouraging children's *positive* behaviors.** Here you will describe how you believe teachers should support and encourage children's positive behaviors. You might talk about providing reinforcement and praise for children who are behaving well. You might discuss being consistent with expectations, so children know what to expect and are more likely to be compliant. You might also explain how rules worded in positive terms, stating ways children *should* be behaving, are more effective than rules that merely state what should *not* be done.

2. **Can you see similarities or differences between your philosophy and the kind of guidance you were given as a child?** Think about how you were parented. Did your parents have an authoritative (democratic) parenting style, using guidance and conversation, or did they have an authoritarian parenting style, using punishment and expecting rigid adherence to rules? Or were you brought up in a permissive home? Do you find yourself aligning with the same guidance principles that your parents used, or is your philosophy different? Explain.

3. **Describe strategies you use to effectively handle children's *challenging* behaviors.** Here you might reflect on how you redirect children, provide alternative activities that may calm them, help them to express anger or frustration in safe ways, provide consistent rules with logical consequences, or any other strategies you would use to help children learn to self-regulate.

Now you have finished all the parts of Competency Statement III. Check the word count, making sure it is right around 500 words. Print this document and place it in the first page protector behind divider E.

You are ready to go on to Competency Statement IV. Start a new page and create a heading:

Competency Statement IV
To establish positive and productive relationships with families

In part 2 of your book, on the "At-A-Glance" chart, you will see that this Competency Standard has only one Functional Area: Families. Your initial paragraph will describe how your teaching practices meet the standard in this Functional Area.

Under the heading you created, write, in bold print, a heading for the Functional Area, followed by your descriptions and examples:

Functional Area 11: Families

You can get some ideas by looking in part 2 of your *Competency Standards* book at the Indicators and Examples provided for Competency Standard IV. However, you may not use these in your own statement. What you write must describe what happens in your particular program. Because there is only one Functional Area, you will need to write quite a few examples to bring your word count up to 500 words.

Describe specific examples of how you develop relationships with the families of the children in your program and encourage their involvement. You might include a discussion about events you have had in the classroom when family volunteers were solicited or any other ways you have found to get families involved in the program, holding parent-teacher conferences, assisting families in crisis with helpful agencies in the community, sharing information about child development with families so they can better understand how their children learn and grow, and similar scenarios.

Looking back at part 1 of the *Competency Standards* book in the Reflective Statements of Competence section, you will see that this statement has three additional parts: CS IV a, CS IV b, and CS IV c. Make a heading for each in bold print:

CS IV a

Explain how you keep families informed about their children's participation in your program on a daily and weekly basis. You might discuss newsletters or other forms of communication you use to connect with families, as well as conferences with families during the year to keep them abreast of their children's progress, strengths, and challenges.

CS IV b

Discuss how you connect with families to gain input about what is happening at home that might be affecting their children. How can this information affect how you interact with and teach children? There are two questions here. First describe how you are able to learn about a child's home life. Again, you may want to talk about having conferences or making time for short, daily chats with families when they arrive in the morning or come to take their children home at the end of the day. The second question asks you to reflect on how knowledge of the different situations in each child's home life will affect how you interact with and teach children.

CS IV c

After reading the Family Questionnaires you distributed and collected, reflect on the feedback the families gave you. Was this feedback expected or surprising compared with what you thought about your own practices? As a result of reading the feedback, were you able to discover a goal for your own professional growth? This will be your own personal reflection on the responses given on the Family Questionnaires. In the past, the questionnaires were not seen by CDA candidates, but the new process values the families' input as an important part of your professional development. As you look at each questionnaire, it will be easy to see what families feel are your strengths, as well as areas you need to work on, which the Council refers to as "areas for future professional growth."

Now you have finished all the parts of Competency Statement IV. Check the word count, making sure it is right around 500 words. Print this document and place it in the first page protector behind divider F.

You are ready to go on to Competency Statement V. Start a new page and create a heading:

Competency Statement V
*To ensure a well-run, purposeful program
that is responsive to participant needs*

In part 2 of your book, on the "At-A-Glance" chart, you will see that this Competency Standard has only one Functional Area: Program Management. Your initial paragraph will describe how your teaching practices meet the standard in this Functional Area.

Under the heading you created, write, in bold print, the heading for this Functional Area, followed by your descriptions and examples:

Functional Area 12: Program Management

You can get some ideas by looking in part 2 of your *Competency Standards* book at the Indicators and Examples provided for Competency Standard V. However, you may not use these in your own statement. What you write must describe what happens in your particular program. Since there is only one Functional Area, you will need to write quite a few examples to bring your word count up to 500 words.

Type a paragraph describing examples of how you promote good program management. You might include such topics as keeping accurate and up-to-date records on each child, providing a family handbook with program policies, holding staff meetings, or providing new employee training.

Looking back at part 1 of the *Competency Standards* book in the Reflective Statements of Competence section, you will see that this statement has one additional part: CS V a. Make a heading for it in bold print:

CS V a

Type a second paragraph about the observation you conducted for the Resource Collection (item RC–V). Describe the type of observation tool and how it was used. Then explain why using observations and documentation are necessary to ensure a well-run program. Finally, explain how you make sure that your observations are accurate and objective and that you are using them to evaluate each child's developmental and learning progress. There are three parts to discuss here. Remember to address all three.

Now you have finished all the parts of Competency Statement V. Check the word count, making sure it is right around 500 words. Print this document and place it in the first page protector behind divider G.

You are ready to go on to Competency Statement VI. Start a new page and create a heading:

Competency Statement VI
To maintain a commitment to professionalism

In part 2 of your book, on the "At-A-Glance" chart, you will see that this Competency Standard has only one Functional Area: Professionalism. Your initial paragraph will describe how your teaching practices meet the standard in this Functional Area. Under the heading you created, write, in bold print, the heading for this Functional Area, followed by your descriptions and examples:

Functional Area 13: Professionalism

You can get some ideas by looking in part 2 of your *Competency Standards* book at the Indicators and Examples provided for Competency Standard VI. However, you may not use these in your own statement. What you write must describe what happens in your particular program. Because there is only one Functional Area, you will need to write quite a few examples to bring your word count up to 500 words.

Write a paragraph describing specific ways you promote professionalism in your program and work. You might mention such things as making sure you maintain confidentiality with families and children, avoiding gossip with coworkers, and taking advantage of professional development opportunities, such as workshops and classes.

Looking back at part 1 of the *Competency Standards* book in the Reflective Statements of Competence section, you will see that this statement has two additional parts: CS VI a and CS VI b. Make headings for them in bold print:

CS VI a

Explain why you have decided to make early childhood education your profession. You will need to reflect on some of your experiences in your past, such as working as a babysitter as a teen, teaching Sunday school, or caring for younger siblings. Try to convey why you feel this profession is a perfect fit for you.

CS VI b

Discuss the qualities you possess that reflect early childhood professionalism. You may want to discuss your commitment to confidentiality with information about children and families in your program. You might also go into detail about the professional development you have participated in within the past year or so. Other topics might include supporting advocacy for quality child care, being knowledgeable about your state's child care regulations, working well with other staff members, being familiar with the NAEYC Code of Ethical Conduct, and similar efforts.

You have finished all the parts of Competency Statement VI. Check the word count, making sure it is right around 500 words. Print this document and place it in the first page protector behind divider H.

This completes your six CDA Competency Statements! Go back to the first page of your Professional Portfolio. On the My CDA Professional Portfolio cover sheet, check off item A, (having this cover sheet in your Portfolio). Go through items C through H, checking off the Reflective Competency Statements.

The next step will be to write your Professional Philosophy Statement.

Writing the Professional Philosophy Statement

Your philosophy statement is a personal reflection of your thoughts on the purposes of education, as well as your educational beliefs, ideals, and values, based upon self-reflection and soul-searching. It should detail your beliefs about how children develop and learn and about what and how they should be taught. Your philosophy will be an ever-changing, evolving document that you update as you grow and develop as an educator.

For your official CDA Professional Philosophy Statement, you will now reflect on each of the following questions, jotting down your ideas on paper. A lot of the preliminary work was already done when you completed the Professional Philosophy Exercise! This part should be easy. Go back to your exercise and use some of the ideas you already wrote down. You should have at least a paragraph for each answer:

- Explain your own attitudes, ideals, and understanding about teaching young children.
- Explain your understanding and viewpoint about how young children learn.
- Discuss how you see yourself as an educator and care provider of young children.
- Reflect on the wider scope of your responsibilities as you interact with and educate the whole child, which encompasses your relationships with families and the community.

Now type the responses to these four questions into a series of paragraphs for your completed CDA Professional Philosophy Statement. The Council does not want this to be more than two pages long. Place the completed document into section I Professional Philosophy Statement, the last section of your Professional Portfolio.

Completing and Submitting the CDA Application

Now that you've completed your training, your Professional Portfolio, and your Professional Philosophy Statement, it's time to submit your application.

Remember, before you apply you must have located and contacted a CDA Professional Development Specialist to conduct your verification visit, because you will need to enter the PD Specialist's identification number on the application form. See chapter 1 for information about locating a PD Specialist.

You can apply online on the Council's website (www .cdacouncil.org/yourcda) or by using the paper application form located at the back of your *Competency Standards* book. It is preferable to use the online option, because it is quicker and any errors or omissions that may have been accidentally made on the application will be discovered immediately and can be corrected right away. With the paper version, mistakes may take time to discover and address, which can hold up the whole process. You will only be given six months to correct any missing or incorrect information on the application form; otherwise, you will forfeit your application fee and have to start the credentialing process all over again.

If you are getting a scholarship or other funding help for the CDA application fee, you will want to check with a staff member at the agency or funder to see how the organization will want your application to be submitted. Some agencies will want a paper application submitted to them, and they will send in the paperwork themselves.

If you are completing the paper application form, be sure to look it over carefully to be certain that all parts have been completed. There are nine parts to the form.

The first part, section A, is for candidate information, such as your name, address, e-mail address, phone number, date of birth, and last four digits of your Social Security number. Most of the fields in this form have a red asterisk, indicating that you are required to complete them.

In section B, you'll indicate the credential type for which you are applying. You will select preschool (three to five years) and indicate the type of program in which you are working (Head Start, private child care, high school vocational, military installation, other).

In section C, you'll indicate in which language you will be taking your CDA Exam and whether you have been granted special accommodations. If you require any special accommodations, such as needing your CDA Exam read to you because of a visual impairment, this must be arranged with the Council prior to your application. If your request is accepted, the Council will provide an approval form that must accompany your application.

Section D provides a form for your payment of the application fee. You can pay by check or money order, but a credit card is preferable because the processing time is much shorter. If an agency is paying this fee, you may have some type of payment authorization letter that will be sent with the application in place of the fee.

Section E is a check-off form in which you will indicate that your required training for a CDA (120 clock hours) has been completed and that your training certificates and transcripts have been placed in the Professional Portfolio, ready for the PD Specialist to review at the verification visit. You *do not* send any of these to the Council with your application.

Section F is a checklist for CDA eligibility, such as the basic education requirements, having a current first-aid/CPR certification, 480 hours of work experience, the majority of the Family Questionnaires collected, and a completed Professional Portfolio. In the space at the bottom of this section, sign and date the page, indicating that the information on the application form is correct, that you will abide by the NAEYC Code of Ethical Conduct and the CDA Standards, and that you have not been convicted of child abuse or neglect (which would make you ineligible for CDA credentialing).

In section G, you'll provide the information about the PD Specialist whom you have contacted and who has agreed to conduct your verification visit. Completion of section H is optional, with spaces for demographic information about race/ethnicity, education, primary/secondary languages, and current position working with children.

Section I is the section for your program director to complete. She will provide her permission for the PD Specialist to come into the program to conduct the classroom observation and the verification visit. The director will also enter information about the program in this section and sign at the bottom.

When this form is completed, look it over once more to be sure all of the sections are complete and that both you and your director have signed it. Then you will mail it to the Council:

The Council for Professional Recognition
2460 16th Street NW
Washington, DC 20009-3547

When the Council accepts the application form, you will receive a Ready to Schedule Notice via the e-mail address you provided on your application form. You then have only six months to complete the CDA Exam and verification visit. After that time, your CDA Candidate Record will be closed. This means you would no longer be on file at the Council and would have to start the whole credentialing process over, including the payment of your application fee.

Now that your application has been submitted and you are waiting for the Ready to Schedule Notice from the Council, this is a good time to prepare for your classroom observation by the PD Specialist. In chapter 8, you will learn how to conduct a self-study of your program environment and practices, using the very same Comprehensive Scoring Instrument that the PD Specialist will use when she comes into your program. The self-study is an extremely valuable exercise and is highly recommended. In addition, take a look at these Program Tips and compare them to your program. These tips are based on the CDA Competency Standards.

Program Tips

The areas in your room should be safe and free from hazards. Good health should be promoted.

- Sharp corners should be covered.

- Flimsy shelving should be removed.

- Electrical cords should be wound up out of reach.

- Miniblind cords should be secured to the tops of windows.

- Small items that could be ingested should not be left out on tables or on the floor.

- Cleaners and chemicals should be secured and locked out of the reach of children.

- Area rugs should be secured to the floor to prevent tripping.

- Caregivers need to wash their hands before handling food, after assisting children in the restroom, and after wiping noses.

- Close supervision should be maintained at all times. Teachers should always position themselves so that they have full view of the room and should never turn their backs on the children.

- The room should be generally clean and tidy.

- Restroom(s) should be sanitized daily. Liquid soap and disposable towels should be available for the children's use.

- Covered, plastic-lined trash cans should be available.

- Children should have separate storage for their own belongings.

- A simple escape route should be posted near the door.

- A chart of CPR and first-aid procedures should be posted.

- A first-aid kit should be readily available in your room. If it is in a cabinet, the outside of the cabinet should be labeled "First-aid" to indicate where it is located.

- At least one fully charged fire extinguisher should be available nearby, and you should be trained in its use.

- Functioning smoke detectors should be installed.

- Good nutrition should be the focus of snacks and meals served. Processed foods and junk foods should not be served. Fruit juice, water, or milk should be the only beverage choices—no Kool-Aid or soda. Teachers should not have sodas or snack foods in the classrooms for themselves.

- When the children eat, the teachers should sit at the tables with them, modeling good table manners, encouraging them to try new foods, and engaging them in pleasant conversation.

Your room should be set up specifically for children.

- There should be a number of "centers" set up for the children. These may include a block area, a dramatic play or housekeeping area, a book corner, and a table or two for creative art or manipulatives.

- There should be ample periods of free-choice time offered daily when children are free to choose among these centers. Children should not be "herded" as a large group from one activity to another. For example, the entire group should not sit down at a table to do an art project. Art should be one of the options for two or three children during free-choice time.

- The surroundings should be bright, cheerful, and inviting to children. There should be lots of the children's art displayed at the children's eye level. Some may be suspended from the ceiling. You may also have interesting posters and mobiles.

- There should be child-sized furniture for the children. This would include tables and chairs.

- There should be age-appropriate toys and materials for preschoolers. These should be stored on low shelves that are easily accessible so the children can easily access and put away the materials.

- There should be opportunities for dramatic play. You may have a child-sized kitchen set, doll beds, dolls, dress-up clothes, and other props.

- There should be a set of building blocks, preferably wood unit blocks, available to the children. The block area should include props, such as small people or animal figures, to encourage creative play.

- Some kind of book corner or shelves should include children's books that they can look at whenever they like. These may be from your own collection or borrowed weekly from the public library. Other literacy materials should also be available as the children show readiness for them, such as child-sized pencils, various types of papers, markers, and washable stamp pads and stamps.

- The environment should be literacy rich. The items in the room should be labeled wherever possible (for example, a small sign on the door that reads "door").

- Children should be read to frequently every day.
- Cultural diversity should be promoted through multiethnic and multiracial dolls and pretend foods of other cultures in the housekeeping area, posters reflecting differences, and a collection of multicultural children's books.
- Both boys and girls should have the opportunity and be encouraged to play in all areas of the room, free from gender bias.
- Adaptations and accommodations should be made for children who have special needs.

There should be opportunities for both large- and small-motor development, as well as cognitive development.

- Age-appropriate manipulatives, puzzles, stacking/sorting toys, interlocking blocks, and playdough should be available.
- There should be a safe place for the children to engage in outdoor play with age-appropriate equipment, such as a climber, swings, a slide, riding toys, and balls.
- Alternative indoor, large-motor activities should be available in case of inclement weather.

Children should have opportunities for creative art on a daily basis, using creative arts materials.

- An easel with paint should be set up.
- Open-ended, process art activities, such as collage, free-form cutting and pasting, or fingerpainting, should be offered. No crafts or coloring book pages should be used.

Children should have the opportunity to learn through play with hands-on activities.

- Learning about colors, for example, should be done by manipulating real items of different colors, not by drills or flash cards.
- Learning shapes and numbers should be done by tactile experiences or games.
- There should be opportunities for many sensory activities, such as cooking, using playdough, handling different textures, and practicing visual discrimination.
- Absolutely no worksheets should be used.
- There should be a variety of age-appropriate toys, materials, and activities.
- Discovery, exploration, and problem solving should be encouraged.
- Children's varied learning styles should be respected and supported by individualizing the activities.

Children should have regular, short, age-appropriate group or circle activities, as well as individual interactions, that encourage socialization between teacher and children and among the children themselves.

- Games should be played.
- Movement activities with or without props or music should be provided.
- Stories should be read on a regular basis.
- Both caregivers and children should have opportunities to engage in storytelling.
- Flannel board stories should be used to provide variety in the presentation of books.
- Fingerplays should be introduced.
- Music should be incorporated into the daily schedule.
- Group activities should not include any type of drills, flash cards, or memorizing.
- No videos or television should be used (or only on rare occasions).

Children should have predictable routines, although daily activities may be flexible to suit the children's needs and interests.

- Greet each child and accompanying adult individually upon arrival.
- Use songs and games to ease transitions from one activity to the next, giving children ample notice when a change is about to occur.
- Have an activity planned for children who finish/transition early, so they do not have to wait for the rest of the group.
- Have daily lesson plans and the materials to carry them out on hand when needed.

Children should be given the opportunity to learn self-discipline in positive, supportive ways.

- Establish a few simple rules with the children. Post them, using pictures to convey ideas. They should be stated in *positive* terms, for example, "Use walking feet," rather than "Don't run."
- Use redirection whenever possible.
- Provide logical and natural consequences for misbehavior.
- Encourage children to use words to convey their feelings.
- Model cooperation, sharing, and proper behavior.
- Use soft voices with the children. Never shout.

- Show ample affection with each child.
- Expect children to help maintain the environment by having them help pick up toys and clean up messes.
- Give children the opportunity to problem solve with each other. Don't be too eager to step in.
- Anticipate problems before they happen, if possible, by being observant.

Interact and play with the children indoors and outdoors.

- Teachers should not be working on lesson plans, cutting things out, chatting with coworkers, or acting otherwise preoccupied while the children are present.
- Be a good listener. Ask lots of open-ended questions and be patient with children as they speak. Spend time talking with each child every day.

Develop a partnership with the families in your program.

- Communicate regularly, verbally and through newsletters and conferences.
- Invite family members to become involved in your program.
- Maintain a family bulletin board with upcoming activities, parenting tips, child development information, and community resources available to them.

Maintain a well-run, organized program.

- Keep up-to-date health and emergency information files on each child in your care.
- Develop a brochure or leaflet for families outlining your center's policies, goals, services offered, and mission statement.
- Take anecdotal notes on each child.
- For each child, keep a portfolio that contains these anecdotal notes, samples of the child's art, and other evidences of skill development that can be shared with parents.

Maintain a commitment to professionalism.

- Join a national or local early childhood organization.
- Observe a strict policy of confidentiality with the families in your program.

Turn to chapter 7 to prepare for the CDA exam and to chapter 8 to read about the verification visit.

The CDA Process: Center-Based Infant/Toddler

Your decision to care for and teach infants or toddlers is an important one. There is an increasing need for skilled and qualified caregivers for this age group. As many as 70 percent of children whose mothers work full-time are in some type of child care. Many of these families now depend on center-based care for their very young children.

Caring for infants and toddlers requires distinct training and skills because of the unique nature of these two age groups. In the past, working with infants and toddlers was viewed as "babysitting," but those who are responsible for the care and education of these children are early childhood professionals, no less than their counterparts working with preschool children. Daily routines constitute the curriculum in the infant or toddler program and are, of necessity, repetitive and constant. This work can, at times, be challenging and demanding on many different levels, requiring a great deal of patience. However, working with these young children is also very rewarding in many ways. These care providers are the ones who witness first steps, hear first words, and form loving attachments with our youngest children.

Care in a group setting is distinctly different from that of preschool children. It is not merely a small-scale form of preschool. Infants and toddlers experience accelerated changes in development and physical growth, more so than at any other time in their lives. These children are also defenseless against harm and distress, and they are totally dependent on their care providers for protection and consistent, loving care.

Part of the work of these professionals is creating strong, reciprocal relationships with families. Optimal growth and development is achieved when close communication and coordination of effort occur between care providers and the children's families (Council for Professional Recognition).

The Child Development Associate (CDA) Competency Standards outline the skills that infant and toddler care providers need to meet the unique needs of these very young children. To get a position in a quality child development center (or to retain the position you already have), to expect advancement, and to demand proper compensation, you are pursuing a CDA Credential and are becoming an early childhood professional. As such, you will need to demonstrate your competency in working with infants and toddlers. Having completed the 120 clock hours of training, you are ready to begin the CDA process. Your Professional Portfolio should now be set up and ready to fill with the Resource Collection.

The Resource Collection

You should already have your Portfolio preliminarily set up, after following the instructions in chapter 3. Next, you will print some one-by-four-inch labels for the dividers to correspond with the small labels on the tabs.

The first divider tab should be labeled **B Family Questionnaires.** Type a one-by-four-inch label with the same information and place it in the center of this divider page. Dividers C through H are for the Competency Statements and Resource Collection items for each of the six Competency Standards.

You will type a one-by-four-inch label to place in the center of each of these tabbed dividers as follows:

C   Tab: **Competency Standard I**
      Label: *Reflective Competency Statement I*
             CS I Resource Collection

D   Tab: **Competency Standard II**
      Label: *Reflective Competency Statement II*
             CS II Resource Collection

E   Tab: **Competency Standard III**
      Label: *Reflective Competency Statement III*
             CS III Resource Collection

F   Tab: **Competency Standard IV**
    Label: *Reflective Competency Statement IV*
          CS IV Resource Collection

G   Tab: **Competency Standard V**
    Label: *Reflective Competency Statement V*
          CS V Resource Collection

H   Tab: **Competency Standard VI**
    Label: *Reflective Competency Statement VI*
          CS VI Resource Collection

The tab on the last divider is labeled **I Professional Philosophy Statement**. Make a one-by-four-inch label with the same information to place in the center of this divider.

Labeling the Page Protectors and Collecting the Resources

You will be using one-by-four-inch labels for the page protectors. Each label will be placed at the upper right corner of a page protector, so it does not obstruct the items placed inside.

    Behind the Summary of My CDA Education cover sheet is an empty page protector. Make a label for it:

Training Certificates/Transcripts

This is the page protector that will hold all of your training certificates and/or transcripts.

    In section B, behind the Family Questionnaires Summary Sheet is an empty page protector. Make a label for it:

Family Questionnaires

This is the page protector that will hold all of your collected Family Questionnaires.

    Now you will be placing page protectors and making labels for each of the Resource Collection items. Some labels have more information to be typed on them than others. You will have to adjust the size of the type you use so that the information will fit on the label.

Begin with section **C Competency Standard I**.

Behind the divider, place four page protectors. For the first page protector, type this label:

Competency Statement I

When you have written your Competency Statement I, it will be placed in this page protector. (Later in this chapter, we will discuss writing the Competency Statements.)

For the second page protector, type this label:

RC I–1
Proof of completion of a first-aid course
and a pediatric CPR course.

Photocopies of your first-aid and CPR course certificates or cards of completion can be placed in the page protector, but you will need the original documents the day of the verification visit. An online course for this training is not acceptable. Training must be from a nationally recognized organization, such as the American Red Cross or the American Heart Association. The certification must be for a *pediatric* CPR course and must be current the day of your verification visit. If it is the wrong type or expired, the CDA process will be stalled until this is corrected.

For the third page protector, type this label:

RC I–2
A menu or feeding plan for young infants,
for mobile infants, and for toddlers.

If you can, provide feeding schedules or menus that you have actually served to children in your program or have created yourself. If this is not possible, you may find some that are appropriate on the Internet. Place the feeding schedules/menus in this page protector. Later, when you write your Competency Statement I, you will be reflecting on the feeding schedules/menus you included here, discussing why you feel they are or are not appropriate for meeting the nutritional needs of infants and toddlers.

For the fourth page protector, type this label:

> ## RC I–3
> ### A weekly plan of learning experiences.

You can use the weekly activity plan form you usually use in your program, perhaps enlarging it to accommodate the information that is required. Be sure to address all of the typical learning areas, such as art, language/literacy, circle, fine- and gross-motor, dramatic play, math, and science. In addition to listing the activities, you need to write the learning goals for each activity, what you expect the children to learn, or how their development will be enhanced by doing the activity. You will indicate the age group for which the plan is intended (young infants, mobile infants, or toddlers). You must also explain if or how each of your activities could be adapted to enable a child who has special needs to participate. This can be for an actual child you have in your program or a fictitious child.

At the top of the weekly plan, indicate the child by first initial and brief statement of the special need:

Children with Special Needs: M. has a visual disability.

Let's say one of your activities is storybook reading. Under that activity you would indicate the accommodation that M. would need in order to participate:

Accommodations: Needs to sit close to the reader, so she can see the pictures.

If no accommodation is needed for a particular activity (listening to a story at circle time, for example), you would indicate this:

Accommodations: None required.

For an example of this, see the Sample Weekly Activity Plans for Infants and for Toddlers that are provided in appendixes D and E. There you will also find a listing of websites that will help you design accommodations for children who have special needs.

Toddler care providers will be sure to address all of the typical learning areas (art, language/literacy, circle, fine- and gross-motor skills, dramatic play, math, science, etc.), while infant care providers will focus on the developmental domains (physical, cognitive, creative, social-emotional) and the daily routines that constitute a typical day.

You have now completed collecting resources for Competency Standard I and are ready to move to section **D Competency Standard II**. Behind the divider, place ten page protectors.

For the first page protector, type this label:

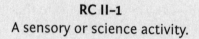

Competency Statement II

When you have written your Competency Statement II, place it in this page protector.

The first group of resources is a collection of activity plans. You will create nine different activities for infants and toddlers. Create three of the activities for young infants, three for mobile infants, and three for toddlers.

For the second page protector, type this label:

RC II–1
A sensory or science activity.

You will create a science or sensory activity. Examples might include a "feely bag" or a blowing bubbles activity.

It is best to use some type of simple activity plan template. On the form, you will indicate the type of activity. For this one, you would indicate "Science or Sensory Activity." You would also indicate for which age group it was intended (young infants, mobile infants, or toddlers), the goal(s) of the activity, the materials needed, the process or procedures, and teaching strategies. Then you will briefly discuss why the activity is developmentally appropriate for that particular age group. See a sample activity plan form provided in appendix C. These activities do not require accommodations.

For the third page protector, type this label:

RC II–2
An activity for language or literacy.

You will create a language or literacy activity. Examples might include reading a story with the children or playing a word game.

Examples are provided solely for the purpose of demonstrating the types of activities that are expected. You need to create your own activities for these Resource Collection items, based on the particular group of children with whom you work.

You will designate for which age this activity is designed. Use the activity plan form.

For the fourth page protector, type this label:

> **RC II–3**
> An activity for creative arts.

You will create a creative arts activity. Examples might include fingerpainting or making a collage. Be sure the activity you create is a "creative" one. You will not want to describe a craft activity that results in some type of product, but rather an activity in which the predominant emphasis is on the process. This will make it easy for you to explain why it is developmentally appropriate. You will designate for which age this activity is designed. Use the activity plan form.

For the fifth page protector, type this label:

> **RC II–4**
> An indoor fine-motor activity.

You will create an indoor fine-motor activity. Examples might include working with playdough or an activity using chubby crayons. You will designate for which age this activity is designed. Use the activity plan form.

For the sixth page protector, type this label:

> **RC II–5**
> An outdoor gross-motor activity.

You will create an outdoor gross-motor activity. Examples might include rolling a ball back and forth with the children or going through an obstacle course of large, soft, foam cubes and a fabric tunnel. You will designate for which age this activity is designed. Use the activity plan form.

For the seventh page protector, type this label:

> **RC II–6**
> An activity that supports children's self-concept.

You will create a self-concept activity. Examples might include looking at oneself in the mirror, sharing a favorite possession at circle time, or singing a song together with the children's names in it. You will designate for which age this activity is designed. Use the activity plan form.

For the eighth page protector, type this label:

RC II–7
An activity that supports children's emotional development or self-regulation.

You will create an emotional skills or self-regulation activity. Examples may include a simple game that requires taking turns or a "Matching Faces" game using photos of people showing different emotions. You will designate for which age this activity is designed. Use the activity plan form.

For the ninth page protector, type this label:

RC II–8
An activity that supports children's development of social skills.

You will create a social skills activity. Examples might include a circle game or an activity that requires children to work in pairs or small groups. You will designate for which age this activity is designed. Use the activity plan form.

For the tenth page protector, type this label:

RC II–9
An activity for math.

You will create a math activity. Examples might include matching number cards or counting and sorting. You will designate for which age this activity is designed. Use the activity plan form.

Place the completed activity plan forms into the labeled page protectors.

You have now completed collecting resources for Competency Standard II and are ready to move to section **E Competency Standard III**. Behind the divider, place two page protectors.

For the first page protector, type this label:

When you have written your Competency Statement III, place it in this page protector.

For the second page protector, type this label:

Each book should be a different title and topic about things related to children's lives and/or situations that may challenge them. These can be books that help children deal with issues such as death, moving to a new home, starting a new school, or a new baby joining the family. They are known as *bibliotherapy* or *therapeutic* books. Or you may choose books about routines or activities children typically experience every day, such as making friends, going to school, or visiting grandparents. Do *not* cut and paste information from an Internet bookstore. These are to be books you have actually used with the children in your program and with which you are very familiar.

If your classroom book collection does not have many or any of these types of books, I would suggest going to the library and bringing back a wide selection that are age and developmentally appropriate for your particular group of children. Then read them to the children. After you do so, these books will qualify to be included in the Resource Collection, because then they are "books you have used with young children."

Type the information requested on one or two pages. Include each book's title, author, copyright date, publisher, and a short summary. Insert the pages back to back into this page protector.

You have now completed collecting resources for Competency Standard III and are ready to move to section **F Competency Standard IV**. Behind the divider, place seven page protectors.

For the first page protector, type this label:

When you have written your Competency Statement IV, place it in this page protector.

The Resource items for this section are a selection of helpful agencies and programs for families. These comprise the Family Resource Guide. The Council asks you to include four specific resources and suggests you locate several more resources in your particular community that would be helpful to families.

For the second page protector, type this label:

> **RC IV–1**
> Information for a local family-counseling agency.

Locate the address, phone number, and website address of the agency. Type the resource information you've found onto a sheet of paper and place it in this page protector.

For the third page protector, type this label:

> **RC IV–2**
> Information about an agency that provides translation services for English as a Second Language (ESL) and for American Sign Language.

This could be one service agency or two. Try to locate agencies in your community that would be easy for families to access. Type this information on a sheet of paper and place in this page protector.

For the fourth page protector, type this label:

> **RC IV–3**
> Information about two or more community agencies that provide services and resources for children who have special needs.

Find information on two or three agencies, which might include those that provide physical therapy, occupational therapy, speech therapy, or developmental or learning services. In some communities, the local school district provides these services. Be sure these are local agencies that families enrolled in your program can access. Include the agencies' names and contact information, along with a short description of the services they provide. Also include information about how families can contact them. Type this information and place it in this page protector.

For the fifth page protector, type this label:

> **RC IV–4**
> Three or more websites, and articles from each,
> that provide families with information about
> children's learning and development.

Type the information about each website, as requested. These websites could include NAEYC (www.naeyc.org), Zero to Three (www.zerotothree.org), Early Childhood News (www.earlychild hoodnews.org), or similar organizations. From each website, download and print one recent article. One of the articles you find must relate to child guidance. Place your typed information and the three articles into this page protector.

For the sixth, seventh, and eighth page protectors, type three of these labels, one for each protector:

> **Additional Helpful Family Resource**

Place these labels on the remaining three empty page protectors. Locate three more helpful resources in your community that would be useful to families. These might include your local agencies that provide food stamps, utility assistance, or child care vouchers. Type the name, description of services provided, and contact information for each agency you found on separate pieces of paper. Place these in the three page protectors labeled "Additional Helpful Family Resource," one page per protector.

You have now completed collecting resources for Competency Standard IV and are ready to move to section **G Competency Standard V**. Behind the divider, place three page protectors.

For the first page protector, type this label:

> **Competency Statement V**

When you have written your Competency Statement V, place it in this page protector.

Remember, you can add even more helpful resources, if you like. Just add more page protectors to hold them. This comprehensive collection of resources will be valuable to you when families are in need of assistance.

For the second page protector, type this label:

> **RC V**
> Three record-keeping forms, including
> a blank accident report, a blank emergency form,
> and a completed observation instrument.

Locate a blank accident report form and a blank emergency form you use in your program. Then you will conduct an observation in your classroom. For the observation tool, you can use the Anecdotal Record Form provided in appendix B. Don't put the child's name on this form—just a first initial would be fine. The observation can be handwritten as long as it is legible. Place these three forms, back to back, in the three page protectors.

You have now completed collecting resources for Competency Standard V and are ready to move to section **H Competency Standard VI**. Behind the divider, place six page protectors.

For the first page protector, type this label:

> **Competency Statement VI**

When you have written your Competency Statement VI, place it in this page protector.

For the second page protector, type this label:

> **RC VI–1**
> The name of and information about
> your state's child care regulatory agency.

Type the name of the agency, its address, and its phone number. You can find your state's child care regulatory agency by going to the National Resource Center for Health and Safety in Child Care and Education website: http://nrckids.org/STATES/states.htm.

Then click on your state and you will find the state licensing contact. Click on the "Regulations" link for child care centers. There you will be able to view and print the sections describing staff, group size, and adult-child ratio requirements that you need to include.

Place the information you typed into this page protector and the sections you printed from the Regulations in the third empty page protector behind it.

For the fourth page protector, type this label:

RC VI–2
Information about two or three
early childhood associations.

These associations may be national, state, regional, or local. They could include the National Association for the Education of Young Children (NAEYC, www.naeyc.org) or the National Association of Child Care Professionals (NACCP, www.naccp .org). Include the web address of each, as well as information about the available professional resources and how to become a member. Type the information and place it in this page protector.

For the fifth page protector, type this label:

RC VI–3
Your state's policies for reporting
child abuse and neglect.

You can find the information about your particular state's policies by going to the Child Welfare Information Gateway (sponsored by the US Department of Health and Human Services) at www.childwelfare.gov/preventing/overview/state.cfm. You will notice you need two pieces of information for this Resource Collection item:

1. Summary of the legal requirements for reporting child abuse and neglect

2. Contact information for the state child abuse/neglect agency in your state (web address, phone number/ address)

Type this information and place it into this page protector.

This completes your Resource Collection! Go to the first page of your Professional Portfolio. On the My CDA Professional Portfolio cover sheet, check off item A, (having this cover sheet in your Portfolio). You will check off item B after you have collected all of your Family Questionnaires. Now go through items C through H, checking off the Resource Collection items for each. You will check off the Reflective Competency Statements for each of these items after they are written. Leave item I unchecked for now, until you write your Professional Philosophy Statement.

Writing the Reflective Statements of Competence

The national Competency Standards are used to evaluate a CDA candidate's skills in working with young children, families, their co-workers, and the community. There are six Competency Standards that define professional caregiver performance. Under each of the Competency Standards are one or more (thirteen in all) Functional Areas. The Functional Areas define, more specifically, the skills and behaviors the candidate must perform to meet each of the Competency Standards. You should read the six Competency Standards with the accompanying Functional Areas in part 2 of your *Competency Standards* book. This information also appears in an "Infant/Toddler Competency Standards At-A-Glance" chart in this section.

You will write six reflections based on your own teaching and interaction with young children, one reflection for each of the six CDA Competency Standards. Each Statement will start with a discussion about how you meet each of the Functional Areas associated with it and then continue with a few other specific reflections, some of which will ask you to comment on items in the Resource Collection. Each statement, including all of its parts, should be no more than 500 words.

We will be looking in two sections of the *Competency Standards* book as you write your Competency Statements:

Part 1: "Earning the Child Development Associate (CDA) Credential" subsection "The Reflective Statements of Competence"

Part 2: "The Child Development Associate Competency Standards"

You will start Competency Statement I by creating a heading:

Competency Statement I
To establish and maintain a safe, healthy learning environment

This will be typed in bold print, with the second line in italics.

In part 2 of your book, on the "At-A-Glance" chart, you will see that this Competency Standard has three Functional Areas: Safe, Healthy, and Learning Environment. Your initial paragraphs will describe how your teaching practices meet this standard in each of the Functional Areas.

Under the heading you created, write, in bold print, headings for the three Functional Areas, followed by your descriptions and examples. You can get some ideas by looking in part 2 of your *Competency Standards* book at the Indicators and Examples provided for Competency Standard I. However, you may not use these in your own statement. What you write must describe what happens in your particular program. Here are examples of what this might look like:

Functional Area 1: Safe

Safety is a main priority in the environment I provide for the children in my care. I make every effort to prevent injuries and accidents. For example, I keep blankets, quilts, and stuffed animals out of cribs to avoid the possibility of suffocation, and I vacuum the carpet frequently to remove small pieces of lint or objects that may be picked up and put in a child's mouth.

Functional Area 2: Healthy

In my program, I encourage and model healthy habits, such as hand washing and covering sneezes and coughs. I also frequently wash all toys that were mouthed by the children, using warm, soapy water and setting them out to air-dry.

Functional Area 3: Learning Environment

I provide developmentally appropriate activities and materials for the children to learn through guided play. Learning materials are kept on low, open shelves so the children can choose for themselves.

Remember, these examples are provided only for clarification and should not be used as part of your own Competency Statements. The examples you write should reflect your particular program, practices, and group of children.

Looking back at part 1 of the *Competency Standards* book in the Reflective Statements of Competence section, you will see that this statement has three additional parts: CS I a, CS I b, and CS I c. Make a heading for each in bold print:

CS I a

Write at least one paragraph reflecting on the sample feeding schedules/menus you placed in your Resource Collection. If you designed the menu, stand behind it and justify your food choices based on your own knowledge and concern about the nutritional needs of children. If you were not the one who designed these but only served the meals, reflect on the strengths and weaknesses you see in the food choices. Discuss what you would change, if anything.

CS I b

Think about the room environment where you will be observed by the PD Specialist. Does this environment represent a place where children can learn best, according to your own philosophy? How? If you were not the one to set up this environment, discuss its strengths and weaknesses. If you had the opportunity, what would you change about it?

In addition, you will also reflect on and describe the differences and similarities between room environments designed for toddlers and those designed for infants.

CS I c

Look at the weekly activity plan you chose for your Resource Collection. Does this plan align with your own philosophy of how children learn best? If you were not the one to create this weekly plan, discuss its strengths and weaknesses. If you had the opportunity, what would you change about it?

Also, explain how you would adapt this weekly plan for use with each of the age groups (young infants, mobile infants, and toddlers).

Now you have finished all the parts of Competency Statement I. Check the word count. If it is fewer than 500 words, add a few more examples for the Functional Areas. If it is more than 500 words, take something out. Print this document and place it in the first page protector behind divider C.

You are ready to go on to Competency Standard II. Start a new page and create a heading:

Competency Standard II
To advance physical and intellectual competence

In part 2 of your book, on the "At-A-Glance" chart, you will see that this Competency Standard has four Functional Areas: Physical, Cognitive, Communication, and Creative. Your initial paragraphs will describe how your teaching practices meet this standard in each of the Functional Areas.

Under the heading you created, write, in bold print, headings for the four Functional Areas:

Functional Area 4: Physical

Functional Area 5: Cognitive

Functional Area 6: Communication

Functional Area 7: Creative

Under each of these headings, you will describe how the Functional Area is met in your program, giving some examples. You can get some ideas by looking in part 2 of your *Competency Standards* book at the Indicators and Examples provided for Competency Standard II. However, you may not use these in your own statement. What you write must describe what happens in your particular program. Here are examples of what this might look like:

Functional Area 4: Physical

In my program, I provide opportunities for children to develop both small- and large-motor skills, and I model enjoyment and active participation in physical activity. On our playground, we have balls and riding toys. Indoors, the children enjoy using playdough and large, plastic snap beads to develop their small muscles.

Functional Area 5: Cognitive

I make available materials and activities that enable children to explore, problem solve, ask questions, and follow their interests. I provide sorting and matching games and ask lots of open-ended questions as they play.

Functional Area 6: Communication

I encourage children to communicate with each other, with me, and with other adults in my program, as well as support their emerging literacy by offering chubby crayons and large sheets of plain paper. I read picture books to them many times during the day. I also label items and areas in the room in both English and Spanish.

Functional Area 7: Creative

I give children opportunities to express their creativity. They experience more process art than assembling products. We have a dramatic play area with props that offer opportunities for make-believe and role play. We also have a large collection of unit blocks for the children to build whatever they like.

Looking back at part 1 of the *Competency Standards* book in the Reflective Statements of Competence section, you will see that this statement has four additional parts: CS II a, CS II b, CS II c, and CS II d. Make a heading for each in bold print:

CS II a

Pick one of the nine learning activities you created for your Resource Collection (RC II). This activity should align with your philosophy of how to best support children's *physical* development. Explain how it does. You will want to choose either the indoor fine-motor activity or the outdoor gross-motor activity, because these support physical development and will be easy to discuss.

CS II b

Pick one of the nine learning activities you created for your Resource Collection (RC II). This activity should align with your philosophy of how to best support children's *cognitive* development. Explain how it does. You will want to choose your science/sensory or your mathematics activity, because these support cognitive development and will be easy to discuss.

CS II c

Pick a third learning experience you created for your Resource Collection (RC II). This activity should align with your philosophy of how to best support children's *creative* development. Explain how it does. You will want to choose your creative arts activity to discuss for this one.

CS II d

Write a paragraph describing how you promote the *language* and *communication* development of all the children in your program, including those who are dual-language learners. For ideas, look in part 2 of the *Competency Standards* book, Competency Standard II (Functional Area 6: Communication). For examples specific to dual-language learners, look in part 3 of the *Competency Standards* book at Principles for Dual Language Learners.

Now you have finished all the parts of Competency Statement II. Check the word count, making sure it is right around 500 words. Print this document and place it in the first page protector behind divider D.

You are ready to go on to Competency Statement III. Start a new page and create a heading:

Competency Statement III
*To support social and emotional development
and to provide positive guidance*

In part 2 of your book, on the "At-A-Glance" chart, you will see that this Competency Standard has three Functional Areas: Self, Social, and Guidance. Your initial paragraphs will describe how your teaching practices meet this standard in each of the Functional Areas.

Under the heading you created, write, in bold print, headings for the three Functional Areas:

Functional Area 8: Self

Functional Area 9: Social

Functional Area 10: Guidance

Under each of these headings, you will describe how the Functional Area is met in your program, giving some examples. You can get some ideas by looking in part 2 of your *Competency Standards* book at the Indicators and Examples provided for Competency Standard III. However, you may not use these in your own statement. What you write must describe what happens in your particular program. Here are examples of what this might look like:

Functional Area 8: Self

I provide opportunities for children to feel independent, successful, and good about themselves. I often use each child's name in songs that I sing. We have photos of the children and their families posted at their eye level in the room. I offer encouragement and praise their efforts.

Functional Area 9: Social

I encourage children to get along with each other and to make friends. I make opportunities for sharing and cooperation through games and activities, and I encourage them to help each other.

If you are a caregiver of infants, you might want to discuss how you take every opportunity to talk and interact with them, while feeding and diapering, for example.

Functional Area 10: Guidance

I use developmentally appropriate strategies to help children learn acceptable behaviors and self-regulation, as well as assisting those who may have more challenging behaviors. I use distraction and redirection whenever possible and take time to talk about what I would like the child to do, rather than what I do not want her to do. I am consistent with my expectations and provide appropriate consequences.

If you are a caregiver of infants, you might want to explain how you respond to their needs promptly, so they learn to trust.

Looking back at part 1 of the *Competency Standards* book in the Reflective Statements of Competence section, you will see that this statement has two additional parts: CS III a and CS III b. Make a heading for each in bold print:

CS III a

Write a paragraph about how you support favorable *self-concepts* and *social-emotional skills* of the children in your program. You will provide specific examples of what you do with children in your program to support these skills. Examples might be providing children encouragement to try things on their own, allowing them to pull up their own clothes after a diaper change, or giving them opportunities to share something special from home at circle time. You might also use examples such as providing opportunities for children to share materials and to play games together.

CS III b

Think about your philosophy of encouraging children's *positive* behaviors. Can you see similarities or differences between your philosophy and the kind of guidance you were given as a child? Then describe strategies you use to effectively handle children's *challenging* behaviors.

Note: You will see that there are three parts to this item. Write a paragraph for each part:

1. **Think about your philosophy of encouraging children's *positive* behaviors.** Here you will describe how you believe teachers should support and encourage children's positive behaviors. You might talk about providing reinforcement and praise for children who are behaving well. You might discuss being consistent with expectations, so children know what to expect and are more likely to be compliant. You might also explain how rules worded in positive terms, stating ways children *should* be behaving, are more effective than rules that merely state what should *not* be done.

2. **Can you see similarities or differences between your philosophy and the kind of guidance you were given as a child?** Think about how you were parented. Did your parents have an authoritative (democratic) parenting style using guidance and conversation, or did they have an authoritarian parenting style, using punishment and expecting rigid adherence to rules? Or were you brought up in a permissive home? Do you find yourself aligning with the same guidance principles that your parents used, or is your philosophy different? Explain.

3. **Describe strategies you use to effectively handle children's *challenging* behaviors.** Here you might reflect on how you distract or redirect children, provide alternative activities that may calm them, help them to express anger or frustration in safe ways, provide consistent rules with logical consequences, or any other strategies you would use to help children learn to self-regulate.

Now you have finished all the parts of Competency Statement III. Check the word count, making sure it is right around 500 words. Print this document and place it in the first page protector behind divider E.

You are ready to go on to Competency Statement IV. Start a new page and create a heading:

Competency Statement IV
To establish positive and productive relationships with families

In part 2 of your book, on the "At-A-Glance" chart, you will see that this Competency Standard has only one Functional Area: Families. Your initial paragraph will describe how your teaching practices meet the standard in this Functional Area.

Under the heading you created, write, in bold print, a heading for the Functional Area, followed by your descriptions and examples:

Functional Area 11: Families

You can get some ideas by looking in part 2 of your *Competency Standards* book at the Indicators and Examples provided for Competency Standard IV. However, you may not use these in your own statement. What you write must describe what happens in your particular program. Because there is only one Functional Area, you will need to write quite a few examples to bring your word count up to 500 words.

Describe specific examples of how you develop relationships with the families of the children in your program and encourage their involvement. You might include a discussion about events you have had in the classroom when family volunteers were solicited or any other ways you have found to get families involved in the program, holding parent-teacher conferences, assisting families in crisis with helpful agencies in the community, sharing information about child development with families so they can better understand how their children learn and grow, and similar scenarios.

Looking back at part 1 of the *Competency Standards* book in the Reflective Statements of Competence section, you will see that this statement has three additional parts: CS IV a, CS IV b, and CS IV c. Make a heading for each in bold print:

CS IV a

Explain how you keep families informed about their child's participation in your program on a daily and weekly basis. You might discuss newsletters, daily sheets, or other forms of communication you use to connect with families, as well as conferences with families during the year to keep them abreast of their children's progress, strengths, and challenges.

CS IV b

Discuss how you connect with families to gain input about what is happening at home that might be affecting their children. How can this information affect how you interact with and teach children? There are two questions here. First describe how you are able to learn about a child's home life. Again, you may want to talk about having conferences or making time for short, daily chats with families when they arrive in the morning or come to take their child home at the end of the day. The second question asks you to reflect on how knowledge of the different situations in each child's home life will affect how you interact with and teach children.

CS IV c

After reading the Family Questionnaires you distributed and collected, reflect on the feedback the families gave you. Was this feedback expected or surprising compared with what you thought about your own practices? As a result of reading the feedback, were you able to discover a goal for your own professional growth? This will be your own personal reflections on the responses given on the Family Questionnaires. In the past, the questionnaires were not seen by CDA candidates, but the new process values the families' input as an important part of your professional development. As you look at each questionnaire, it will be easy to see what families feel are your strengths, as well as areas you need to work on, which the Council refers to as "areas for future professional growth."

Now you have finished all the parts of Competency Statement IV. Check the word count, making sure it is right around 500 words. Print this document and place it in the first page protector behind divider F.

You are ready to go on to Competency Statement V. Start a new page and create a heading:

Competency Statement V
To ensure a well-run, purposeful program
that is responsive to participant needs

In part 2 of your book, on the "At-A-Glance" chart, you will see that this Competency Standard has only one Functional Area: Program Management. Your initial paragraph will describe how your teaching practices meet the standard in this Functional Area.

Under the heading you created, write, in bold print, the heading for this Functional Area, followed by your descriptions and examples:

Functional Area 12: Program Management

You can get some ideas by looking in part 2 of your *Competency Standards* book at the Indicators and Examples provided for Competency Standard V. However, you may not use these in your own statement. What you write must describe what happens in your particular program. Since there is only one Functional Area, you will need to write quite a few examples to bring your word count up to 500 words.

Type a paragraph describing examples of how you promote good program management. You might include such topics as keeping accurate and up-to-date records on each child, providing a family handbook with program policies, holding staff meetings, or providing new employee training.

Looking back at part 1 of the *Competency Standards* book in the Reflective Statements of Competence section, you will see that this Statement has one additional part: CS V a. Make a heading for it in bold print:

CS V a

Type a second paragraph about the observation you conducted for the Resource Collection (item RC–V). Describe the type of observation tool and how it was used. Then explain why using observations and documentation are necessary to ensure a well-run program. Finally, explain how you make sure that your observations are accurate and objective and that you are using them to evaluate each child's developmental and learning progress. There are three parts to discuss here. Remember to address all three.

Now you have finished all the parts of Competency Statement V. Check the word count, making sure it is right around 500 words. Print this document and place it in the first page protector behind divider G.

You are ready to go on to Competency Statement VI. Start a new page and create a heading:

Competency Statement VI
To maintain a commitment to professionalism

In part 2 of your book, on the "At-A-Glance" chart, you will see that this Competency Standard has only one Functional Area: Professionalism. Your initial paragraph will describe how your teaching practices meet the standard in this Functional Area. Under the heading you created, write, in bold print, the heading for this Functional Area, followed by your descriptions and examples:

Functional Area 13: Professionalism

You can get some ideas by looking in part 2 of your *Competency Standards* book at the Indicators and Examples provided for Competency Standard VI. However, you may not use these in your own statement. What you write must describe what happens in your particular program. Because there is only one Functional Area, you will need to write quite a few examples to bring your word count up to 500 words.

Write a paragraph describing specific ways you promote professionalism in your program and work. You might mention such things as making sure you maintain confidentiality with families and children, avoiding gossip with coworkers, and taking advantage of professional development opportunities, such as workshops and classes.

Looking back at part 1 of the *Competency Standards* book in the Reflective Statements of Competence section, you will see that this statement has two additional parts: CS VI a and CS VI b. Make headings for them in bold print:

CS VI a

Explain why you have decided to make early childhood education your profession. You will need to reflect on some of your experiences in your past, such as working as a babysitter as a teen, teaching Sunday school, or caring for younger siblings. Try to convey why you feel this profession is a perfect fit for you.

CS VI b

Discuss the qualities you possess that reflect early childhood professionalism. You may want to discuss your commitment to confidentiality with information about children and families in your program. You might also go into detail about the professional development you have participated in within the past year or so. Other topics might include supporting advocacy for quality child care, being knowledgeable about your state's child care regulations, working well with other staff members, being familiar with the NAEYC Code of Ethical Conduct, and similar efforts.

You have finished all the parts of Competency Statement VI. Check the word count, making sure it is right around 500 words.

Print this document and place it in the first page protector behind divider H.

This completes your six CDA Competency Statements! Go back to the first page of your Professional Portfolio. On the My CDA Professional Portfolio cover sheet, check off item A (having this cover sheet in your Portfolio). Go through items C through H, checking off the Reflective Competency Statements.

The next step will be to write your Professional Philosophy Statement.

Writing the Professional Philosophy Statement

Your philosophy statement is a personal reflection of your thoughts on the purposes of education, as well as your educational beliefs, ideals, and values, based upon self-reflection and soul-searching. It should detail your beliefs about how children develop and learn and about what and how they should be taught. Your philosophy will be an ever-changing, evolving document that you update as you grow and develop as an educator.

For your official CDA Professional Philosophy Statement, you will now reflect on each of the following questions, jotting down your ideas on paper. A lot of the preliminary work was already done when you completed the Professional Philosophy Exercise! This part should be easy. Go back to your exercise and use some of the ideas you already wrote down. You should have at least a paragraph for each answer:

- Explain your own attitudes, ideals, and understanding about teaching young children.

- Explain your understanding and viewpoint about how young children learn.

- Discuss how you see yourself as an educator and care provider of young children.

- Reflect on the wider scope of your responsibilities as you interact with and educate the whole child, which encompasses your relationships with families and the community.

Now type these responses to these four questions into a series of paragraphs for your completed CDA Professional Philosophy Statement. The Council does not want this to be more than two pages long. Place the completed document into section I Professional Philosophy Statement, the last section of your Professional Portfolio.

Completing and Submitting the CDA Application

Now that you've completed your training, your Professional Portfolio, and your Professional Philosophy Statement, it's time to submit your application.

Remember, before you apply you must have located and contacted a CDA Professional Development Specialist to conduct your verification visit, because you will need to enter the PD Specialist's identification number on the application form. See chapter 1 for information about locating a PD Specialist.

You can apply online on the Council's website (www .cdacouncil.org/yourcda) or by using the paper application form located at the back of your *Competency Standards* book. It is preferable to use the online option, because it is quicker and any errors or omissions that may have been accidentally made on the application will be discovered immediately and can be corrected right away. With the paper version, mistakes may take time to discover and address, which can hold up the whole process. You will only be given six months to correct any missing or incorrect information on the application form; otherwise, you will forfeit your application fee and have to start the credentialing process all over again.

If you are getting a scholarship or other funding help for the CDA application fee, you will want to check with a staff member at the agency or funder to see how the organization will want your application to be submitted. Some agencies will want a paper application submitted to them, and they will send in the paperwork themselves.

If you are completing the paper application form, look it over carefully to be certain all parts have been completed. There are nine parts to the form.

The first part, section A, is for candidate information, such as your name, address, e-mail address, phone number, date of birth, and last four digits of your Social Security number. Most of the fields in this form have a red asterisk, indicating that you are required to complete them.

In section B, you'll indicate the credential type for which you are applying. You will select infant/toddler and indicate the type of program in which you are working (Head Start, private child care, high school vocational, military installation, other).

In section C, you'll indicate in which language you will be taking your CDA Exam and whether you have been granted special accommodations. If you require any special accommodations, such as needing your CDA Exam read to you because of a visual impairment, this must be arranged with the Council prior to your application. If your request is accepted, the Council will provide an approval form that must accompany your application.

Section D provides a form for your payment of the application fee. You can pay by check or money order, but a credit card is preferable because the processing time is much shorter. If an agency is paying this fee, you may have some type of payment authorization letter that will be sent with the application in place of the fee.

Section E is a check-off form in which you will indicate that your required training for a CDA (120 clock hours) has been completed and that your training certificates and transcripts have been placed in the Professional Portfolio, ready for the PD Specialist to review at the verification visit. You *do not* send any of these to the Council with your application.

Section F is a checklist for CDA eligibility, such as the basic education requirements, having a current first-aid/CPR certification, 480 hours of work experience, the majority of the Family Questionnaires collected, and a completed Professional Portfolio. In the space at the bottom of this section, sign and date the page, indicating that the information on the application form is correct, that you will abide by the NAEYC Code of Ethical Conduct and the CDA Standards, and that you have not been convicted of child abuse or neglect (which would make you ineligible for CDA credentialing).

In section G, you'll provide the information about the PD Specialist whom you have contacted and who has agreed to conduct your verification visit. Completion of section H is optional, with spaces for demographic information about race/ethnicity, education, primary/secondary languages, and current position working with children.

Section I is the section for your program director to complete. She will provide her permission for the PD Specialist to come into the program to conduct the classroom observation and the verification visit. The director will also enter information about the program in this section and sign at the bottom.

When this form is completed, look it over once more to be sure all of the sections are complete and that both you and your director have signed it. Then you will mail it to the Council:

The Council for Professional Recognition
2460 16th Street NW
Washington, DC 20009-3547

When the Council has accepted your application form, you will receive a Ready to Schedule Notice via the e-mail address you provided on your application form. You then have only six months to complete the CDA Exam and verification visit. After that time, your CDA Candidate Record will be closed. This means you would no longer be on file at the Council and would have to start the whole credentialing process over, including the payment of your application fee.

Now that your application has been submitted and you are waiting for the Ready to Schedule Notice from the Council, this is a good time to prepare for your classroom observation by the PD Specialist. In chapter 8, you will learn how to conduct a self-study of your program environment and practices, using the very same Comprehensive Scoring Instrument that the PD Specialist will use when she comes into your program. The self-study is an extremely valuable exercise and is highly recommended. In addition, take a look at these Program Tips and compare them to your program. These tips are based on the CDA Competency Standards.

Program Tips

The areas in your room should be safe and free from hazards. Good health should be promoted.

- Sharp corners should be covered.

- Flimsy shelving should be removed.

- Electrical cords should be wound up and out of reach.

- Miniblind cords should be secured to the tops of windows.

- Small items that could be ingested should not be left out on tables or on the floor.

- Cleaners and chemicals should be secured and locked out of the reach of children.

- Area rugs should be secured to the floor to prevent tripping.

- Caregivers need to wash their hands before handling food, after assisting children in the restroom, and after wiping noses.

- Toys should be continually washed and sanitized throughout the day as they are "mouthed" by the children.

- High chairs are washed and sanitized after each use, including the seat, frame, and tray.

- Close supervision should be maintained at all times. Teachers should always position themselves so they have full view of the room and should never turn their backs on the children.

- The room should be generally clean and tidy.

- Restroom(s) should be sanitized daily. Liquid soap and disposable towels should be available for the children's use, as well as low sinks, so toddlers can learn to wash their hands independently.

- Covered, plastic-lined trash cans should be available, one specifically for soiled diapers. Remove the soiled diapers often, so there is never an odor permeating the diapering area or room.

- Be familiar with and use safe sleeping positions with infants: either side or back placement.

- Keep blankets, quilts, and toys out of cribs.

- Children should be fully attended on a changing table. Make sure all supplies needed are within reach prior to beginning a diaper change.

- Make sure there are no cracks or tears on the surface of the changing table pad, even if a sheet of paper is used under the child when diapering. Do not use any type of tape in an attempt to repair it. Just replace it.

- Label each child's box of moist diaper wipes and diaper rash cream with the child's name to avoid cross-contamination.

- Children should have separate storage for their own belongings. Never store belongings in a child's crib.

- A simple escape route should be posted near the door.

- A chart of CPR and first-aid procedures should be posted.

- A first-aid kit should be readily available in your room. If it is in a cabinet, the outside of the cabinet should be labeled "First-aid" to indicate where it is located.

- At least one fully charged fire extinguisher should be available nearby, and you should be trained in its use.

- Functioning smoke detectors should be installed.

- Good nutrition should be the focus of snacks and meals served. Processed foods and junk foods should not be served. Fruit juice, water, or milk should be the only beverage choices—no Kool-Aid or soda. Teachers should not have sodas or snack foods in the classrooms for themselves.

- When the children eat, the teachers should sit at the tables with them, modeling good table manners, encouraging them to try new foods, and engaging them in pleasant conversation.

- Keep each child's formula labeled in the refrigerator. Half-used bottles or baby food jars should not be sitting around the room, but should be discarded promptly after feeding.

- Infants are held for feedings. They should not be in an infant seat or crib with a propped bottle at any time.

Your room should be set up specifically for children.

- There should be a number of "centers" set up for the children. These may include a block area, a dramatic play or housekeeping area, a book corner, and a table or two for creative art or manipulatives.

- There should be ample periods of free-choice time offered daily when children are free to choose among these centers. Children should not be "herded" as a large group from one activity to another. For example, the entire group should not sit down at a table to do an art project. Art should be one of the options for two or three children during free-choice time.

- The surroundings should be bright, cheerful, and inviting to children. There should be lots of the children's art displayed at the children's eye level. Some items may be suspended from the ceiling. You may also have interesting posters and mobiles hanging.

- There should be child-sized furniture for the children. This would include tables and chairs.

- There should be age-appropriate toys and materials for young infants, mobile infants, or toddlers, depending on the age group in your care. These should be stored on low shelves so that the children can easily access and put away the materials.

- Provide duplicates of popular toys to discourage conflicts.

- There should be opportunities for dramatic play. You may have a child-sized kitchen set, doll beds, dolls, dress-up clothes, and other props.

- There should be a set of building blocks, preferably wood unit blocks, available to the children. The block area should include props, such as people or animal figures, to encourage creative play.

- Some kind of book corner or shelves should include cloth and board books that very young children can look at whenever they like. These books may be from your own collection or borrowed weekly from the public library. Other literacy materials should be made available as the children show readiness for them, such as child-sized pencils, various types of papers, washable markers, and chubby crayons.

- The environment should be literacy rich. The items in the room should be labeled wherever possible (for example, a small sign on the door that reads "door").

- Children should be read to frequently every day.

- Include a variety of music in the environment, including singing.

- Spend time with individual children, on their level, at every opportunity, engaging them in play.

- Move nonmobile infants to different areas of the room throughout the day, changing their positions and perspectives.
- Provide safe, open floor space for exploration and movement.
- Provide items that encourage independence for toddlers, such as step stools at the sink and Velcro closures on paint smocks.
- Talk with individual children as you work through their daily routines, encouraging them to listen and respond. Use these times as opportunities for verbal interaction and bonding.
- Practice primary caregiving whenever possible.
- Cultural diversity should be promoted through multiethnic and multiracial dolls and pretend foods of other cultures in the housekeeping area, posters reflecting differences, and a collection of multicultural children's books.
- Both boys and girls should have opportunity and be encouraged to play in all areas of the room, free from gender bias.
- Adaptations and accommodations should be made for children who have special needs.

There should be opportunities for both large- and small-motor development, as well as cognitive development.

- Age-appropriate manipulatives, puzzles, stacking/sorting toys, interlocking blocks, and playdough should be available.
- There should be a safe place for the children to engage in outdoor play with age-appropriate equipment, such as a climber, swings, a slide, riding toys, and balls.
- Infants should be provided with time outdoors whenever weather permits.
- Alternate indoor, large-motor activities should be available in case of inclement weather.
- Infants should be given periods of "tummy time" every day on a floor surface under close supervision.

Children should have opportunities for creative activities on a daily basis, using creative arts materials.

- An easel with paint should be set up.
- Open-ended, process art activities, such as collage, free-form cutting and pasting, or fingerpainting, should be offered. No crafts or coloring book pages should be allowed.
- Infants should be provided with objects to bat and kick and toys that respond to touch and movement.

Children should have the opportunity to learn through play, with hands-on activities.

- Learning about colors, for example, should be done by manipulating real items of different colors, not by drills or flash cards.
- Learning shapes and numbers should be done by tactile experiences or games, not through flash cards or drills.
- There should be opportunities for many sensory activities, such as cooking, using playdough, handling different textures, and practicing visual discrimination.
- Absolutely no worksheets should be used.
- Discovery, exploration, and problem solving should be encouraged.
- Children's varied learning styles and abilities should be respected and supported by individualizing the activities.

Children should have regular, short, age-appropriate group or circle activities and individual interactions that encourage socialization between teacher and children and among the children themselves.

- Games should be played.
- Movement activities with or without props or music should be provided.
- Stories should be read on a regular basis.
- Both caregivers and children should have opportunities to engage in storytelling.
- Flannel board stories should be used to provide variety in the presentation of books.
- Fingerplays should be introduced.
- Music should be incorporated into the daily schedule.
- Group activities should not include any type of drills, flash cards, or memorizing.
- No videos or television should be allowed.
- Cribs should be used only for sleeping. Infants should be out of the crib when awake, being held by the caregiver, placed in a swing for short periods, or positioned on a prepared area of the floor to play and exercise.
- Infant seats, bouncers, and mechanical swing devices should not be overused or used as a substitute for human contact.

Children should have predictable routines, although daily activities may be flexible to suit the children's needs and interests.

- Greet each child and accompanying adult individually upon arrival.

- Use songs and games to ease transitions from one activity to the next, giving children ample notice when a change is about to occur.
- Have an activity planned for children who finish/transition early, so they do not have to wait for the rest of the group.
- Create a weekly activity plan for toddlers, based on their daily routines.
- Create a daily activity plan for each infant, based on individual schedule and needs. Infants should not have their schedules altered, such as being awakened from a nap to take a walk in the stroller.

Children should be given the opportunity to learn self-discipline in positive, supportive ways.

- Establish a few simple rules with the children. Post them, using pictures to convey ideas. They should be stated in positive terms, for example, "Use walking feet," rather than "Don't run."
- Use redirection whenever possible with toddlers.
- Provide logical and natural consequences for misbehavior.
- Encourage children to use words to convey their feelings.
- Model cooperation, sharing, and proper behavior.
- Use soft voices with the children. Never shout.
- Show ample affection with each child.
- Expect children to help maintain the environment by having them help pick up toys and clean up messes.
- Give children the opportunity to problem solve with each other. Don't be too eager to step in.
- Anticipate problems before they happen, if possible, by being observant.

Interact and play with the children indoors and outdoors.

- Teachers should not be working on lesson plans, cutting things out, chatting with coworkers, or acting otherwise preoccupied while the children are present.
- Upon waking, infants should be responded to promptly and taken from their cribs.
- Be a good listener. Ask lots of open-ended questions and be patient with children as they try to respond and speak. Spend time talking with each child every day.

Develop a partnership with the families in your program.

- Communicate regularly, verbally and through newsletters and conferences.
- Invite family members to become involved in your program.

Turn to chapter 7 to prepare for the CDA exam and to chapter 8 to read about the verification visit.

• Maintain a family bulletin board with upcoming activities, parenting tips, child development information, and community resources available to them.

Maintain a well-run, organized program.

• Keep up-to-date health and emergency information files on each child in your care.

• Develop a brochure or leaflet for families outlining your center's policies, goals, services offered, and mission statement.

• Take anecdotal notes on each child.

• For each child, keep a portfolio that contains these anecdotal notes, samples of the child's art, and other evidences of skill development that can be shared with parents.

Maintain a commitment to professionalism.

• Join a national or local early childhood organization.

• Observe a strict policy of confidentiality with the families in your program.

• Continue to improve your skills by attending workshops or classes.

The CDA Process: Family Child Care

Family child care comes in many forms, from a provider working on her own to a group of providers operating an organized agency of in-home programs. A person who chooses to provide family child care can specialize in part-time or full-time care, twenty-four-hour care, infant care, or care for mixed ages. Often, family child care providers decide on this type of care because they want to stay at home with their own children or they want the flexibility of providing the type of care they prefer. They sometimes have an assistant or two, depending on the number of children in their care.

Family child care is usually more informal and flexible than center-based programs, and it provides a setting similar to what children would experience in their own homes. Also, family child care typically serves smaller groups of children, so more opportunity exists for individualized care and interaction. All in all, family child care comes in as many forms as there are family child care providers.

The typical family child care provider cares for a multiage group, with children between the ages of birth and five years, although she may care for school-age children for part of the day, as well.

This type of care can be very challenging. The care provider must divide her time among many tasks and roles. She will cook, play, clean, teach, and socialize. She will need special skills and knowledge about the development of children at different ages to provide appropriate activities and care and to meet their individual needs. In addition, she will need skills in running her home business, including marketing and record keeping. A family child care program is often funded solely by the payments made to the provider by the parents, but many times there is additional funding from federal, state, or county programs or agencies in the form of subsidies, which requires yet additional bookkeeping and management skills.

In spite of the challenges and demands of the work, family child care is also very rewarding for those who choose to do it. These providers have the opportunity to form warm, loving relationships with young children, who often remain in the program for a number of years prior to going to school and may even continue on an after-school basis thereafter. Family child care providers have the satisfaction of operating their own programs in their own homes, many of whom are also caring for their own children at the same time.

The Child Development Associate (CDA) Competency Standards were developed to evaluate family child care programs for quality and competent care. The Competency Standards outline the specific skills providers should have to meet the needs of the children, whether they are infants, toddlers, or preschoolers. The Standards do not expect family child care programs to be set up or run like child care centers. They recognize the unique nature of family child care, with its flexible schedule and routines and the varied personalities and visions of the individuals who provide the care.

Look over the *Competency Standards* book from the Council, and you will see six Competency Standards upon which you will be evaluated. You will need to complete several tasks in the process toward your credential, which may, at first glance, appear to be quite a challenge. However, if you take them one step at a time, you will find the process not only well within your capability, but also a very rewarding experience. As such, you will need to demonstrate your competency in working with infants, toddlers, and preschoolers. Having completed the 120 clock hours of training, you are ready to begin the CDA process. Your Professional Portfolio should now be set up and ready to fill with the Resource Collection.

The Resource Collection

You should already have your Portfolio preliminarily set up, after following the instructions in chapter 3. Next, you will print some one-by-four-inch labels for the dividers to correspond with the small labels on the tabs.

The first divider tab should be labeled **B Family Questionnaires.** Type a one-by-four-inch label with the same information and place it in the center of this divider page. Dividers

C through H are for the Competency Statements and Resource Collection items for each of the six Competency Standards.

You will type a one-by-four-inch label to place in the center of each of these tabbed dividers as follows:

C Tab: **Competency Standard I**
   Label: *Reflective Competency Statement I*
   CS I Resource Collection

D Tab: **Competency Standard II**
   Label: *Reflective Competency Statement II*
   CS II Resource Collection

E Tab: **Competency Standard III**
   Label: *Reflective Competency Statement III*
   CS III Resource Collection

F Tab: **Competency Standard IV**
   Label: *Reflective Competency Statement IV*
   CS IV Resource Collection

G Tab: **Competency Standard V**
   Label: *Reflective Competency Statement V*
   CS V Resource Collection

H Tab: **Competency Standard VI**
   Label: *Reflective Competency Statement VI*
   CS VI Resource Collection

The tab on the last divider is labeled **I Professional Philosophy Statement.** Make a one-by-four-inch label with the same information to place in the center of this divider.

Labeling the Page Protectors and Collecting the Resources

You will be using one-by-four-inch labels for the page protectors. Each label will be placed at the upper right corner of a page protector, so it does not obstruct the items placed inside.

Behind the Summary of My CDA Education cover sheet is an empty page protector. Make a label for it:

Training Certificates/Transcripts

This is the page protector that will hold all of your training certificates and/or transcripts.

In section B, behind the Family Questionnaires Summary Sheet, is an empty page protector. Make a label for it:

Family Questionnaires

This is the page protector that will hold all of your collected Family Questionnaires.

Now you will be placing page protectors and making labels for each of the Resource Collection items. Some labels have more information to be typed on them than others. You will have to adjust the size of the type you use so that the information will fit on the label.

Begin with section **C Competency Standard I**.

Behind the divider, place four page protectors. For the first page protector, type this label:

Competency Statement I

When you have written your Competency Statement I, it will be placed in this page protector. (Later in this chapter, we will discuss writing the Competency Statements.)

For the second page protector, type this label:

RC I–1
Proof of completion of a first-aid course
and a pediatric CPR course.

Photocopies of your first-aid and CPR course certificates or cards of completion can be placed in the page protector, but you will need the original documents the day of the verification visit. An online course for this training is not acceptable. Training must be from a nationally recognized organization, such as the American Red Cross or the American Heart Association. The certification must include a *pediatric* CPR course and must be current the day of your verification visit. If it is the wrong type or expired, the CDA process will be stalled until this is corrected.

For the third page protector, type this label:

> ### RC I–2
> A one-week family child care menu.

If you can, provide a menu that you have actually served to children in your program or have created yourself. If this is not possible, you may find one that is appropriate on the Internet. Place the menu in this page protector. Later, when you write your Competency Statement I, you will be reflecting on the menu you included here, discussing why you feel it is or is not appropriate for meeting the nutritional needs of young children.

For the fourth page protector, type this label:

> ### RC I–3
> A weekly plan of learning experiences.

You can use the weekly activity plan form you usually use in your program, perhaps enlarging it to accommodate the information that is required. Be sure to address all of the typical learning areas, such as art, language/literacy, circle, fine- and gross-motor skills, dramatic play, math, and science. In addition to listing the activities, you need to write the learning goals for each activity, what you expect the children to learn, or how their development will be enhanced by doing the activity. You will indicate the age group for which the plan is intended (infants, toddlers, or preschoolers). You must also explain if or how each of your activities could be adapted to enable a child who has special needs to participate. This can be for an actual child you have in your program or a fictitious child.

At the top of the weekly plan, indicate the child by first initial and brief statement of the special need:

Children with Special Needs: M. has a visual disability.

Let's say one of your activities is storybook reading. Under that activity you would indicate the accommodation that M. would need to participate:

Accommodations: Needs to sit close to the reader, so she can see the pictures.

If no accommodation is needed for a particular activity (listening to a story at circle time, for example), you would indicate this:

Accommodations: None required.

For an example of this, see the Sample Weekly Activity Plans for Toddlers and for Infants and for Preschool that are provided in appendixes C and D. There you will also find a listing of websites that will help you design accommodations for children with special needs.

Toddler and preschool care providers will be sure to address all of the typical learning areas (art, language/literacy, circle, fine- and gross-motor skills, dramatic play, math, science). Infant care providers will focus on the developmental domains (physical, cognitive, creative, social-emotional) and the daily routines that constitute a typical day.

You have now completed collecting resources for Competency Standard I and are ready to move to section **D Competency Standard II**. Behind the divider, place ten page protectors.

For the first page protector, type this label:

Competency Statement II

Examples are provided solely for the purpose of demonstrating the types of activities that are expected. You need to create your own activities for these Resource Collection items, based on the particular group of children with whom you work.

When you have written your Competency Statement II, place it in this page protector.

The first group of resources is a collection of activity plans. You will create nine different activities for infants, toddlers, and preschoolers. Create three of the activities for infants, three for toddlers, and three for preschoolers.

For the second page protector, type this label:

RC II–1
A sensory or science activity.

You will create a science or sensory activity. Examples might include a "feely bag" or a blowing bubbles activity.

It is best to use some type of simple activity plan template. On the form, you will indicate the type of activity it is. For this one, you would write "Science or Sensory Activity." You would also indicate for which age group it was intended (infants, toddlers, or preschoolers), the goal(s) of the activity, the materials needed, the process or procedures, and teaching strategies. Then you will briefly discuss why the activity is developmentally appropriate for that particular age group. Use the sample activity plan form provided in appendix C.

For the third page protector, type this label:

> ### RC II–2
> An activity for language or literacy.

You will create a language or literacy activity. Examples might include reading a story with the children or playing a word game. You will designate for which age this activity is designed. Use the activity plan form.

For the fourth page protector, type this label:

> ### RC II–3
> An activity for creative arts.

You will create a creative arts activity. Examples might include fingerpainting or making a collage. Be sure the activity you create is a "creative" one. You will not want to describe a craft activity that results in some type of product, but rather an activity in which the predominant emphasis is on the process. This will make it easy for you to explain why it is developmentally appropriate. You will designate for which age this activity is designed. Use the activity plan form.

For the fifth page protector, type this label:

> ### RC II–4
> An indoor fine-motor activity.

You will create an indoor fine-motor activity. Examples might include working with playdough or an activity using chubby crayons. You will designate for which age this activity is designed. Use the activity plan form.

For the sixth page protector, type this label:

> ### RC II–5
> An outdoor gross-motor activity.

You will create an outdoor gross-motor activity. Examples might include rolling a ball back and forth with the children or going through an obstacle course of large, soft foam cubes and a fabric tunnel. You will designate for which age this activity is designed. Use the activity plan form.

For the seventh page protector, type this label:

> **RC II–6**
> An activity that supports children's self-concept.

You will create a self-concept activity. Examples might include looking at oneself in the mirror, sharing a favorite possession at circle time, or singing a song together with the children's names in it. You will designate for which age this activity is designed. Use the activity plan form.

For the eighth page protector, type this label:

> **RC II–7**
> An activity that supports children's
> emotional development or self-regulation.

You will create an emotional skills or self-regulation activity. Examples may include a simple game that requires taking turns or a "Matching Faces" game using photos of people showing different emotions. You will designate for which age this activity is designed. Use the activity plan form.

For the ninth page protector, type this label:

> **RC II–8**
> An activity that supports children's
> development of social skills.

You will create a social skills activity. Examples might include a circle game or an activity that requires children to work in pairs or small groups. You will designate for which age this activity is designed. Use the activity plan form.

For the tenth page protector, type this label:

> **RC II–9**
> An activity for math.

You will create a math activity. Examples might include matching number cards or counting and sorting. You will designate for which age this activity is designed. Use the activity plan form.

Place the completed activity plan forms into the labeled page protectors.

You have now completed collecting resources for Competency Standard II and are ready to move to section **E Competency Standard III**. Behind the divider, place two page protectors.

For the first page protector, type this label:

Competency Statement III

When you have written your Competency Statement III, place it in this page protector.

For the second page protector, type this label:

RC III
A bibliography of ten developmentally
appropriate children's books.

Each book should be a different title and topic about things related to children's lives or situations that may challenge them. These can be books that help children deal with issues such as death, moving to a new home, starting a new school, or a new baby joining the family. They are known as *bibliotherapy* or *therapeutic* books. Or you may choose books about routines or activities children typically experience every day, such as making friends, going to school, or visiting grandparents. Do *not* cut and paste information from an Internet bookstore. These are to be books you have actually used with the children in your program and with which you are very familiar.

If your classroom book collection does not have many or any of these types of books, I would suggest going to the library and bringing back a wide selection that are age and developmentally appropriate for your particular group of children. Then read them to the children. After doing so, these books will qualify to be included in the Resource Collection, because then they are "books you have used with young children."

Type the information requested on one or two pages. Include each book's title, author, copyright date, publisher, and a short summary. Insert the pages back to back in this page protector.

You have now completed collecting resources for Competency Standard III and are ready to move to section **F Competency Standard IV**. Behind the divider, place seven page protectors.

For the first page protector, type this label:

> **Competency Statement IV**

When you have written your Competency Statement IV, place it in this page protector.

The Resource Collection items for this section are a selection of helpful agencies and programs for families. These comprise the Family Resource Guide. The Council asks you to include four specific resources and suggests you locate several more resources in your particular community that would be helpful to families.

For the second page protector, type this label:

> **RC IV–1**
> Information for a local family-counseling agency.

Locate the address, phone number, and website address of the agency. Type the resource information you've found onto a sheet of paper and place it in this page protector.

For the third page protector, type this label:

> **RC IV–2**
> Information about an agency that provides translation services for English as a Second Language (ESL) and for American Sign Language.

This could be one service agency or two. Try to locate agencies in your community that would be easy for families to access. Type this information on a sheet of paper and place it in this page protector.

For the fourth page protector, type this label:

> **RC IV–3**
> Information about two or more community agencies that provide services and resources for children who have special needs.

Find information about two or three agencies, which might include those that provide physical therapy, occupational therapy, speech therapy, or developmental or learning services. In some communities, the local school district provides these services. Be sure these are local agencies that families enrolled in your program can access. Include the agencies' names and contact information, along with a short description of the services they provide. Type this information and place it in this page protector.

For the fifth page protector, type this label:

> **RC IV–4**
> Three or more websites, and articles from each, that provide families with information about children's learning and development.

Remember, you can add even more helpful resources, if you like. Just add more page protectors to hold them. This comprehensive collection of resources will be valuable to you when families are in need of assistance.

Type the information about each website, as requested. These websites could include those for NAEYC (www.naeyc.org), Zero to Three (www.zerotothree.org), Early Childhood News (www.earlychildhoodnews.org), or similar organizations. From each website, download and print one recent article. One of the articles you find must relate to child guidance. Place your typed information and the three articles into this page protector.

For the sixth, seventh, and eighth page protectors, type three labels with this phrase, one for each protector:

> **Additional Helpful Family Resource**

Place these labels on the remaining three empty page protectors. Locate three more helpful resources in your community that would be useful to families. These might include your local agencies that provide food stamps, utility assistance, or child care vouchers. Type the name, description of services provided, and contact information for each agency you found on separate pieces of paper. Place these in the three page protectors labeled "Additional Helpful Family Resource," one page per protector.

You have now completed collecting resources for Competency Standard IV and are ready to move to section **G Competency Standard V.** Behind the divider, place three page protectors.

For the first page protector, type this label:

Competency Statement V

When you have written your Competency Statement V, place it in this page protector.

For the second page protector, type this label:

RC V
Three record-keeping forms, including
a blank accident report, a blank emergency form,
and a completed observation tool.

Locate a blank accident report form and a blank emergency form you use in your program. Then you will conduct an observation in your classroom. For the observation tool, you can use the Anecdotal Record Form provided in appendix B. Don't put the child's name on this form—just a first initial would be fine. The observation can be handwritten as long as it is legible. Place these three forms, back to back, in the three page protectors.

You have now completed collecting resources for Competency Standard V and are ready to move to section **H Competency Standard VI**. Behind the divider, place six page protectors.

For the first page protector, type this label:

Competency Statement VI

When you have written your Competency Statement VI, place it in this page protector.

For the second page protector, type this label:

RC VI–1
The name of and information about
your state's child care regulatory agency.

Type the name of the agency, its address, and its phone number. You can find your state's child care regulatory agency by going to the National Resource Center for Health and Safety in Child Care and Education website: http://nrckids.org/STATES/states.htm.

Then click on your state and you will find the state licensing contact. Click on the "Regulations" link for child care centers. There you will be able to view and print the sections describing the qualification requirements for personnel (teachers, directors, and assistants), group size, and adult-child ratio requirements.

Place the information you typed into this page protector and the sections you printed from the Regulations in the third empty page protector behind it.

For the fourth page protector, type this label:

> **RC VI–2**
> Information about two or three
> early childhood associations.

These associations may be national, state, regional, or local. They could include the National Association for the Education of Young Children (NAEYC, www.naeyc.org) or the National Association of Child Care Professionals (NACCP, www.naccp.org). Include the web address of each, as well as information about the available professional resources and how to become a member. Type the requested information about the organizations you choose. Place it in this page protector.

For the fifth page protector, type this label:

> **RC VI–3**
> Your state's policies for reporting
> child abuse and neglect.

You can find the information about your particular state's policies by going to the Child Welfare Information Gateway (sponsored by the US Department of Health and Human Services) at www .childwelfare.gov/preventing/overview/state.cfm. You will notice you need two pieces of information for this Resource Collection item:

1. Summary of the legal requirements for reporting child abuse and neglect

2. Contact information for the state child abuse/neglect agency in your state (web address, phone number/ address)

Type this information and place it into this page protector.

This completes your Resource Collection! Go to the first page of your Professional Portfolio. On the My CDA Professional Portfolio cover sheet, check off item A (having this cover sheet in your Portfolio). You will check off item B after you have collected all of your Family Questionnaires. Now go through items C through H, checking off the Resource Collection items for each. You will check off the Reflective Competency Statements for each of these items after they are written. Leave item I unchecked for now, until you write your Professional Philosophy Statement.

Writing the Reflective Statements of Competence

The national Competency Standards are used to evaluate a CDA candidate's skills in working with young children, families, their coworkers, and the community. There are six Competency Standards that define professional caregiver performance. Under each of the Competency Standards are one or more (thirteen in all) Functional Areas. The Functional Areas define, more specifically, the skills and behaviors the candidate must perform to meet each of the Competency Standards. You should read over the six Competency Standards with the accompanying Functional Areas in part 2 of your *Competency Standards* book. This information also appears in a "Family Child Care Competency Standards At-A-Glance" chart in this section.

You will write six reflections based on your own teaching and interaction with young children, one reflection for each of the six CDA Competency Standards. Each statement will start with a discussion about how you meet each of the Functional Areas associated with it and then continue with a few other specific reflections, some of which will ask you to comment on items in the Resource Collection. Each statement, including all of its parts, should be no more than 500 words.

We will be looking in two sections of the *Competency Standards* book as you write your Competency Statements:

Part 1: "Earning the Child Development Associate (CDA) Credential" subsection "The Reflective Statements of Competence"

Part 2: "The Child Development Associate Competency Standards"

You will start Competency Statement I by creating a heading:

Competency Statement I
To establish and maintain a safe, healthy learning environment

This will be typed in bold print, with the second line in italics.

In part 2 of your book, on the "At-A-Glance" chart, you will see that this Competency Standard has three Functional Areas: Safe, Healthy, and Learning Environment. Your initial paragraphs will describe how your teaching practices meet this standard in each of the Functional Areas.

Under the heading you created, write, in bold print, the headings for the three Functional Areas, followed by your descriptions and examples. You can get some ideas by looking in part 2 of your *Competency Standards* book at the Indicators and Examples provided for Competency Standard I. However, you may not use these in your own statement. What you write must describe what happens in your particular program. Here are examples of what this might look like:

Remember, these examples are provided only for clarification and should not be used as part of your own Competency Statements. The examples you write should reflect your particular program, practices, and group of children.

Functional Area 1: Safe

Safety is a main priority in the environment I provide for the children in my care. I make every effort to prevent injuries and accidents. For example, I keep blankets, quilts, and stuffed animals out of cribs to avoid the possibility of suffocation, and I vacuum the carpet frequently to remove small pieces of lint or objects that may be picked up and put in a child's mouth.

Functional Area 2: Healthy

In my program, I encourage and model healthy habits, such as hand washing and covering sneezes and coughs. I also frequently wash all toys that were mouthed by the children in warm, soapy water and set them out to air-dry.

Functional Area 3: Learning Environment

I provide developmentally appropriate activities and materials for the children to learn through guided play. Learning materials are kept on low, open shelves so the children can choose for themselves.

Looking back at part 1 of the *Competency Standards* book in the Reflective Statements of Competence section, you will see that this statement has three additional parts: CS I a, CS I b, and CS I c. Make a heading for each in bold print:

CS I a

Write at least one paragraph reflecting on the sample menu you placed in your Resource Collection. If you designed the menu, stand behind it and justify your food choices based on your own commitment to children's nutritional needs. If you were not the one who designed the menu but only served the meals, reflect on the strengths and weaknesses you see in the food choices. Discuss what you would change, if anything.

CS I b

Think about the room environment where you will be observed by the PD Specialist. Does this environment represent a place where children can learn best, according to your own philosophy? How? If you were not the one to set up this environment, discuss its strengths and weaknesses. If you had the opportunity, what would you change about it?

CS I c

Look back at the weekly activity plan you chose for your Resource Collection. Does this plan align with your own philosophy of how children learn best? If you were not the one to create this weekly plan, discuss its strengths and weaknesses. If you had the opportunity, what would you change about it?

Now you have finished all the parts of Competency Statement I. Check the word count. If it is fewer than 500 words, add a few more examples for the Functional Areas. If it is more than 500 words, take something out. Print this document and place it in the first page protector behind divider C.

You are ready to go on to Competency Standard II. Start a new page and create a heading:

Competency Standard II
To advance physical and intellectual competence

In part 2 of your book, on the "At-A-Glance" chart, you will see that this Competency Standard has four Functional Areas: Physical, Cognitive, Communication, and Creative. Your initial paragraphs will describe how your teaching practices meet this standard in each of the Functional Areas.

Under the heading you created, write, in bold print, headings for the four Functional Areas:

Functional Area 4: Physical

Functional Area 5: Cognitive

Functional Area 6: Communication

Functional Area 7: Creative

Under each of these headings, you will describe how the Functional Area is met in your program, giving some examples.

You can get some ideas by looking in part 2 of your *Competency Standards* book at the Indicators and Examples provided for Competency Standard II. However, you may not use these in your own statement. What you write must describe what happens in your particular program. Here are examples of what this might look like:

Functional Area 4: Physical
In my program, I provide opportunities for children to develop both small- and large-motor skills, and I model enjoyment and active participation in physical activity. On our playground, we have balls and riding toys. Indoors, the children enjoy using playdough and large, plastic snap beads to develop their small muscles.

Functional Area 5: Cognitive
I make available materials and activities that enable children to explore, problem solve, ask questions, and follow their interests. I provide sorting and matching games, and I ask lots of open-ended questions as they play.

Functional Area 6: Communication
I encourage children to communicate with each other, with me, and with other adults in my program, as well as support their emerging literacy by offering chubby crayons and large sheets of plain paper. I read picture books to them many times during the day. I also label items and areas in the room in both English and Spanish.

Functional Area 7: Creative
I give children opportunities to express their creativity. They experience more process art than assembling products. We have a dramatic play area with props that offer opportunities for make-believe and role play. We also have a large collection of unit blocks for the children to build whatever they like.

Looking back at part 1 of the *Competency Standards* book in the Reflective Statements of Competence section, you will see that this statement has four additional parts: CS II a, CS II b, CS II c, and CS II d. Make a heading for each in bold print:

CS II a

Pick one of the nine learning activities you created for your Resource Collection (RC II). This activity should align with your philosophy of how to best support children's *physical* development.

Explain how it does. You will want to choose either the indoor fine-motor activity or the outdoor gross-motor activity, because these support physical development and will be easy to discuss.

CS II b

Pick one of the nine learning activities you created for your Resource Collection (RC II). This activity should align with your philosophy of how to best support children's *cognitive* development. Explain how it does. You will want to choose your science/sensory or your mathematics activity, because these support cognitive development and will be easy to discuss.

CS II c

Pick a third learning activity you created for your Resource Collection (RC II). This activity should align with your philosophy of how to best support children's *creative* development. Explain how it does. You will want to choose your creative arts activity to discuss for this one.

CS II d

Write a paragraph describing how you promote the *language* and *communication* development of all the children in your program, including those who are dual-language learners. For ideas, look in part 2 of the *Competency Standards* book, Competency Standard II (Functional Area 6: Communication). For examples specific to dual-language learners, look in part 3 of the *Competency Standards* book at Principles for Dual Language Learners.

Now you have finished all the parts of Competency Statement II. Check the word count, making sure it is right around 500 words. Print this document and place it in the first page protector behind divider D.

You are ready to go on to Competency Statement III. Start a new page and create a heading:

Competency Statement III
*To support social and emotional development
and to provide positive guidance*

In part 2 of your book, on the "At-A-Glance" chart, you will see that this Competency Standard has three Functional Areas: Self, Social, and Guidance. Your initial paragraphs will describe how your teaching practices meet this standard in each of the Functional Areas.

Under the heading you created, write, in bold print, headings for the three Functional Areas:

Functional Area 8: Self

Functional Area 9: Social

Functional Area 10: Guidance

Under each of these, you will describe how the Functional Area is met in your program, giving some examples. You can get some ideas by looking in part 2 of your *Competency Standards* book at the Indicators and Examples provided for Competency Standard III. However, you may not use these in your own statement. What you write must describe what happens in your particular program. Here are examples of what this might look like:

Functional Area 8: Self

I provide opportunities for children to feel independent, successful, and good about themselves. I often use each child's name in songs that I sing. We have photos of the children and their families posted at their eye level in the room. I offer encouragement and praise their efforts.

Functional Area 9: Social

I encourage children to get along with each other and make friends. I make opportunities for sharing and cooperation through games and activities, and I encourage them to help each other.

Functional Area 10: Guidance

I use developmentally appropriate strategies to help children learn acceptable behaviors and self-regulation, as well as assisting those who may have more challenging behaviors. I use distraction and redirection whenever possible, and I take time to talk about what I would like the child to do, rather than what I do not want her to do. I am consistent with my expectations and provide appropriate consequences.

Looking back at part 1 of the *Competency Standards* book in the Reflective Statements of Competence section, you will see that this statement has two additional parts: CS III a and CS III b. Make a heading for each in bold print:

CS III a

Write a paragraph about how you support favorable *self-concepts* and *social-emotional skills* of the children in your program. You will provide specific examples of what you do with children in your program to support these skills. Examples might be providing children encouragement to try things on their own, allowing them to print their own names on their projects, or giving them opportunities to share something special from home at circle time. You might also use examples such as providing opportunities for children to share materials and to play games together.

CS III b

Think about your philosophy of encouraging children's *positive* behaviors. Can you see similarities or differences between your philosophy and the kind of guidance you were given as a child? Then describe strategies you use to effectively handle children's *challenging* behaviors.

Note: You will see that are three parts to this item. Write a paragraph for each part:

1. **Think about your philosophy of encouraging children's *positive* behaviors.** Here you will describe how you believe teachers should support and encourage children's positive behaviors. You might talk about providing reinforcement and praise for children who are behaving well. You might discuss being consistent with expectations, so children know what to expect and are more likely to be compliant. You might also explain how rules worded in positive terms, stating ways children *should* be behaving, are more effective than rules that merely state what should *not* be done.

2. **Can you see similarities or differences between your philosophy and the kind of guidance you were given as a child?** Think about how you were parented. Did your parents have an authoritative (democratic) parenting style using guidance and conversation, or did they have an authoritarian parenting style, using punishment and expecting rigid adherence to rules? Or were you brought up in a permissive home? Do you find yourself aligning with the same guidance principles that your parents used, or is your philosophy different? Explain.

3. **Describe strategies you use to effectively handle children's *challenging* behaviors.** Here you might reflect on how you distract or redirect children, provide alternative activities that may calm them, help them to express anger or frustration in safe ways, provide consistent rules with logical consequences, or any other strategies you would use to help children learn to self-regulate.

Now you have finished all the parts of Competency Statement III. Check the word count, making sure it is right around 500 words. Print this document and place it in the first page protector behind divider E.

You are ready to go on to Competency Statement IV. Start a new page and create a heading:

Competency Statement IV
To establish positive and productive relationships with families

In part 2 of your book, on the "At-A-Glance" chart, you will see that this Competency Standard has only one Functional Area: Families. Your initial paragraph will describe how your teaching practices meet the standard in this Functional Area.

Under the heading you created, write, in bold print, the heading for the Functional Area, followed by your descriptions and examples:

Functional Area 11: Families

You can get some ideas by looking in part 2 of your *Competency Standards* book at the Indicators and Examples provided for Competency Standard IV. However, you may not use these in your own statement. What you write must describe what happens in your particular program. Since there is only one Functional Area, you will need to write quite a few examples to bring your word count up to 500 words.

Describe specific examples of how you develop relationships with the families of the children in your program and encourage their involvement. You might include a discussion about events you have had in the classroom when family volunteers were solicited or any other ways you have found to get families involved in the program, holding parent-teacher conferences, assisting families in crisis with helpful agencies in the community, sharing information about child development with families so they can better understand how their children learn and grow, and similar scenarios.

Looking back at part 1 of the *Competency Standards* book in the Reflective Statements of Competence section, you will see that this statement has three additional parts: CS IV a, CS IV b, and CS IV c. Make a heading for each in bold print:

CS IV a

Explain how you keep families informed about their children's participation in your program on a daily and weekly basis. You might discuss newsletters, daily sheets, or other forms of communication you use to connect with families, as well as conferences with families during the year to keep them abreast of their children's progress, strengths, and challenges.

CS IV b

Discuss how you connect with families to gain input about what is happening at home that might be affecting their children. How can this information affect how you interact with and teach children? There are two questions here. First describe how you are able to learn about a child's home life. Again, you may want to talk about having conferences or making time for short, daily chats with families when they arrive in the morning or come to take their child home at the end of the day. The second question asks you to reflect on how knowledge of the different situations in each child's home life will affect your teaching practices.

CS IV c

After reading the Family Questionnaires you distributed and collected, reflect on the feedback the families gave you. Was this feedback expected or surprising compared with what you thought about your own practices? As a result of reading these, were you able to discover a goal for your own professional growth? This will be your own personal reflections on the responses given on the Family Questionnaires. In the past, the questionnaires were not seen by CDA candidates, but the new process values the families' input as an important part of your professional development. As you look at each questionnaire, it will be easy to see what families feel are your strengths, as well as areas you need to work on, which the Council refers to as "areas for future professional growth."

Now you have finished all the parts of Competency Statement IV. Check the word count, making sure it is right around 500 words. Print this document and place it in the first page protector behind divider F.

You are ready to go on to Competency Statement V. Start a new page and create a heading:

Competency Statement V
To ensure a well-run, purposeful program
that is responsive to participant needs

In part 2 of your book, on the "At-A-Glance" chart, you will see that this Competency Standard has only one Functional Area: Program Management. Your initial paragraph will describe how your teaching practices meet the standard in this Functional Area.

Under the heading you created, write, in bold print, the heading for this Functional Area, followed by your descriptions and examples:

Functional Area 12: Program Management

You can get some ideas by looking in part 2 of your *Competency Standards* book at the Indicators and Examples provided for Competency Standard V. However, you may not use these in your own statement. What you write must describe what happens in your particular program. Since there is only one Functional Area, you will need to write quite a few examples to bring your word count up to 500 words.

Type a paragraph describing examples of how you promote good program management. You might include such topics as keeping accurate and up-to-date records on each child, providing a family handbook with program policies, holding staff meetings, or providing new employee training.

Looking back at part 1 of the *Competency Standards* book in the Reflective Statements of Competence section, you will see that this statement has one additional part: CS V a. Make a heading for it in bold print:

CS V a

Type a second paragraph about the observation you conducted for the Resource Collection (item RC–V). Describe the type of observation tool and how it was used. Then explain why using observations and documentation are necessary to ensure a well-run program. Finally, explain how you make sure that your observations are accurate and objective and that you are using them to evaluate each child's developmental and learning progress. There are three parts to discuss here. Remember to address all three.

Now you have finished all the parts of Competency Statement V. Check the word count, making sure it is right around 500 words. Print this document and place it in the first page protector behind divider G.

You are ready to go on to Competency Statement VI. Start a new page and create a heading:

Competency Statement VI
To maintain a commitment to professionalism

In part 2 of your book, on the "At-A-Glance" chart, you will see that this Competency Standard has only one Functional Area: Professionalism. Your initial paragraph will describe how your teaching practices meet the standard in this Functional Area.

Under the heading you created, write, in bold print, the heading for this Functional Area, followed by your descriptions and examples:

Functional Area 13: Professionalism

You can get some ideas by looking in part 2 of your *Competency Standards* book at the Indicators and Examples provided for Competency Standard VI. However, you may not use these in your own statement. What you write must describe what happens in your particular program. Since there is only one Functional Area, you will need to write quite a few examples to bring your word count up to 500 words.

Write a paragraph describing specific ways you promote professionalism in your program and work. You might mention such things as making sure you maintain confidentiality with families and children, avoiding gossip with coworkers, and taking advantage of professional development opportunities, such as workshops and classes.

Looking back at part 1 of the *Competency Standards* book in the Reflective Statements of Competence section, you will see that this statement has two additional parts: CS VI a and CS VI b. Make headings for them in bold print:

CS VI a

Explain why you have decided to make early childhood education your profession. You will need to reflect on some of your experiences in your past, such as working as a babysitter as a teen, teaching Sunday school, or caring for younger siblings. Try to convey why you feel this profession is a perfect fit for you.

CS VI b

Discuss the qualities you possess that reflect early childhood professionalism. You may want to discuss your commitment to confidentiality with information about children and families in your program. You might also go into detail about the professional development you have participated in within the past year or so. Other topics might include supporting advocacy for quality child care, being knowledgeable about your state's child care regulations, working well with other staff members, being familiar with the NAEYC Code of Ethical Conduct, and similar efforts.

You have finished all the parts of Competency Statement VI. Check the word count, making sure it is right around 500 words. Print this document and place it in the first page protector behind divider H.

This completes your six CDA Competency Statements! Go back to the first page of your Professional Portfolio. On the My

CDA Professional Portfolio cover sheet, check off item A, (having this cover sheet in your Portfolio). Go through items C through H, checking off the Reflective Competency Statements.

The next step will be to write your Professional Philosophy Statement.

Writing the Professional Philosophy Statement

Your philosophy statement is a personal reflection of your thoughts on the purposes of education, as well as your educational beliefs, ideals, and values, based upon self-reflection and soul-searching. It should detail your beliefs about how children develop and learn and about what and how they should be taught. Your philosophy will be an ever-changing, evolving document that you update as you grow and develop as an educator.

For your official CDA Professional Philosophy Statement, you will now reflect on each of the following questions, jotting down your ideas on paper. A lot of the preliminary work was already done when you completed the Professional Philosophy Exercise! This part should be easy. Go back to your exercise and use some of the ideas you already wrote down. You should have at least a paragraph for each answer:

- Explain your own attitudes, ideals, and understanding about teaching young children.

- Explain your understanding and viewpoint about how young children learn.

- Discuss how you see yourself as an educator and care provider of young children.

- Reflect on the wider scope of your responsibilities as you interact with and educate the whole child, which encompasses your relationships with families and the community.

Now type the responses to these four questions into a series of paragraphs for your completed CDA Professional Philosophy Statement. The Council does not want this to be more than two pages long. Place the completed document into section I, Professional Philosophy Statement, the last section of your Professional Portfolio.

Completing and Submitting the CDA Application

Now that you've completed your training, your Professional Portfolio, and your Professional Philosophy Statement, it's time to submit your application.

Remember, before you apply you must have located and contacted a CDA Professional Development Specialist to conduct your verification visit, because you will need to enter the PD Specialist's identification number on the application form. See chapter 1 for information about locating a PD Specialist.

You can apply online on the Council's website (www .cdacouncil.org/yourcda) or by using the paper application form located at the back of your *Competency Standards* book. It is preferable to use the online option, because it is quicker and any errors or omissions that may have been accidentally made on the application will be discovered immediately and can be corrected right away. With the paper version, mistakes may take time to discover and address, which can hold up the whole process. You will only be given six months to correct any missing or incorrect information on the application form; otherwise, you will forfeit your application fee and have to start the credentialing process all over again.

If you are getting a scholarship or other funding help for the CDA application fee, you will want to check with a staff member at the agency or funder to see how the organization will want your application to be submitted. Some agencies will want a paper application submitted to them, and they will send in the paperwork themselves.

If you are completing the paper application form, be sure to look it over carefully to be sure all parts have been completed. There are nine parts to the form.

The first part, section A, is for candidate information, such as your name, address, e-mail address, phone number, date of birth, and last four digits of your Social Security number. Most of the fields in this form have a red asterisk, indicating that you are required to complete them.

In section B, you indicate the credential type for which you are applying. You will check Family Child Care (birth to five years) and will check the same in the section asking for your type of program.

In section C, you'll indicate in which language you will be taking your CDA Exam and whether you have been granted special accommodations. If you require any special accommodations, such as needing your CDA Exam read to you because of a visual impairment, this must be arranged with the Council prior to your application. If your request is accepted, the Council will provide an approval form that must accompany your application.

Section D provides a form for your payment of the application fee. You can pay by check or money order, but a credit card is preferable because the processing time is much shorter. If an agency is paying this fee, you may have some type of payment authorization letter that will be sent with the application in place of the fee.

Section E is a check-off form in which you will indicate that your required training for a CDA (120 clock hours) has been completed and that your training certificates and transcripts have been placed in the Professional Portfolio, ready for the PD Specialist to review at the verification visit. You *do not* send any of these to the Council with your application.

Section F is a checklist for CDA eligibility, such as the basic education requirements, having a current first-aid/CPR certification, 480 hours of work experience, the majority of the Family Questionnaires collected, and a completed Professional Portfolio. In the space at the bottom of this section, sign and date the page, indicating that the information on the application form is correct, that you will abide by the NAEYC Code of Ethical Conduct and the CDA Standards, and that you have not been convicted of child abuse or neglect (which would make you ineligible for CDA credentialing).

In section G, you'll provide the information about the PD Specialist whom you have contacted and who has agreed to conduct your verification visit. Completion of section H is optional, with spaces for demographic information about race/ethnicity, education, primary/secondary languages, and current position working with children.

Section I is the section for you to enter information about the family child care program. If you are the program owner, you will check the boxes under "Director Statement" and sign at the bottom of this section. If you are an employee at the family child care program, have the owner check off the items and sign.

When this form is completed, look it over once more to be sure all of the sections are complete and that you have signed it. Then you will mail it to the Council:

The Council for Professional Recognition
2460 16th Street NW
Washington, DC 20009-3547

When the Council has accepted your application form, you will receive a Ready to Schedule Notice via the e-mail address you provided on your application form. You then have only six months to complete the CDA Exam and verification visit. After that time, your CDA Candidate Record will be closed. This means you would no longer be on file at the Council and would have to start the whole credentialing process over, including the payment of your application fee. If you provided an e-mail address on the application, the Council will send reminders to schedule the CDA Exam and verification visit, but don't rely on these. Be responsible for scheduling and completing the process on your own!

Now that your application has been submitted and you are waiting for the Ready to Schedule Notice from the Council, this is a good time to prepare for your observation by the PD Specialist. In chapter 8, you will learn how to conduct a self-study of your program environment and practices, using the very same Comprehensive Scoring Instrument that the PD Specialist will use when she comes into your program. The self-study is an extremely valuable exercise and is highly recommended. In addition, take a look at these Program Tips and compare them to your program. These tips are based on the CDA Competency Standards.

Program Tips

The areas in your room should be safe and free from hazards. Good health should be promoted.

- Sharp corners should be covered.

- Flimsy shelving and furniture should be removed.

- Electrical cords should be wound up and out of reach.

- Miniblind cords should be secured to the tops of windows.

- Small items that could be ingested should not be left out on tables or on the floor.

- Household cleaning supplies, prescription medication and other drugs, and houseplants should be kept secured and locked out of reach.

- Precautions should be taken when the stove is in use. Safety latches are used on drawers and cabinets.

- Area rugs should be secured to the floor to prevent tripping.

- Caregivers need to wash their hands before handling food, after assisting children in the restroom, and after wiping noses.

- Close supervision should be maintained at all times. Care providers should always position themselves so they have full view of the room and should never turn their backs on the children.

- The room should be generally clean and tidy.

- Accommodations should be made for different developmental stages, such as the use of safety gates and outlet covers.

- Restroom(s) should be sanitized daily. Liquid soap and disposable towels should be available for the children's use.
- Covered, plastic-lined trash cans should be available.
- Children should have separate storage for their own belongings.
- A simple escape route should be posted near the door.
- A chart of CPR and first-aid procedures should be posted.
- A first-aid kit should be readily available. If it is in a cabinet, the outside of the cabinet should be labeled "First-aid" to indicate where it is located.
- At least one fully charged fire extinguisher should be available nearby, and you should be trained in its use.
- Functioning smoke detectors should be installed.
- Good nutrition should be the focus of snacks and meals served. Processed foods and junk foods should not be served. Fruit juice, water, or milk should be the only beverage choices—no Kool-Aid or soda. Caregivers should not have sodas or snack foods in the classrooms for themselves.
- When the children eat, the care providers should sit at the tables with them, modeling good table manners, encouraging them to try new foods, and engaging them in pleasant conversation.
- Include the children, when possible, in the preparation of food for the group or in helping with simple household chores.

The area(s) of your home designated for child care should be set up specifically for children.

- Provide a good variety of materials and toys that are easily accessible to the children, which will encourage them to put items away themselves.
- Take advantage of neighborhood opportunities, such as parks, a public library, gardens, snowy hills, or friendly neighbors.
- There should be child-sized furniture for the children. This would include tables and chairs.
- Organize play areas within the home so similar activities are adjacent to each other, younger children have protected areas in which to play, and older children can use materials suited to their developmental levels without interruption.
- There should be opportunities for dramatic play. You may have a child-sized kitchen set, doll beds, dolls, dress-up clothes, and other props. Safe, household items should be available, such as pots, pans, lids, and plastic cups.
- There should be a set of building blocks, preferably wood unit blocks, available to the children. The block area should include

props, such as small people or animal figures, to encourage creative play.

- Some kind of book corner or shelves should include children's books that they can look at whenever they like. These may be from your own collection or borrowed weekly from the public library. Other literacy materials should also be available as the children show readiness for them, such as child-sized pencils, various types of papers, markers, washable stamp pads, and stamps.

- The environment should be literacy rich. The items in the room should be labeled wherever possible (for example, a small sign on the door that reads "door").

- Children should be read to frequently every day.

- Cultural diversity should be promoted through multiethnic and multiracial dolls and pretend foods of other cultures for dramatic play, posters reflecting differences, and a collection of multicultural children's books.

- Both boys and girls should have the opportunity and be encouraged to play in all areas, free from gender bias.

- Adaptations and accommodations should be made for children who have special needs.

- There should be opportunities for older and younger children to play together.

There should be opportunities for both large- and small-motor development, as well as cognitive development.

- Age-appropriate manipulatives, puzzles, stacking and sorting toys, interlocking blocks, playdough, and simple, homemade materials should be available for play.

- There should be a safe place for the children to engage in outdoor play, with age-appropriate equipment, such as a climber, swings, a slide, riding toys, and balls.

- There should be alternative indoor, large-motor activities available in case of inclement weather.

Children should have opportunities for creative activities on a daily basis, using creative art materials.

- Paints, crayons, colored chalk, and markers should be readily available.

- Open-ended, process art activities, such as collage, free-form cutting and pasting, or fingerpainting should be offered. No crafts or coloring book pages should be used.

Children should have the opportunity to learn through play, with hands-on activities.

- Learning about colors, for example, should be done by manipulating real items of different colors, not by drills or flash cards.
- Learning shapes and numbers should be done by tactile experiences or games, not through flash cards or drills.
- There should be opportunities for many sensory activities, such as cooking, using playdough, handling different textures, and practicing visual discrimination.
- Absolutely no worksheets should be used.
- There should be a variety of age-appropriate toys, materials, and activities.
- Discovery, exploration, and problem solving should be encouraged.
- Children's varied learning styles are respected and supported.

Children should have regular, short, age-appropriate group or circle activities as well as individual interactions that encourage socialization between teacher and children and among the children themselves.

- Games should be played.
- Movement activities with or without props or music should be provided.
- Stories should be read on a regular basis.
- Both caregivers and children should have opportunities to engage in storytelling.
- There should be very limited use of videos or television.
- Flannel board stories should be used to provide variety in the presentation of books.
- Fingerplays should be introduced.
- Music should be incorporated into the daily schedule.
- Group activities should not include any type of drills, flash cards, or memorizing.

Children should have predictable routines, although daily activities may be flexible to suit the children's needs and interests.

- Greet each child and accompanying adult individually upon arrival.
- Use songs and games to ease transitions from one activity to the next, giving children ample notice when a change is about to occur.

- Have an activity planned for children who finish/transition early, so they do not have to wait for the rest of the group.
- Have daily lesson plans and the materials to carry them out on hand when needed.

Children should be given the opportunity to learn self-discipline in positive, supportive ways.

- Establish a few simple rules with the children. Post them, using pictures to convey ideas. They should be stated in positive terms, for example, "Use walking feet," rather than "Don't run."
- Use redirection whenever possible.
- Provide logical and natural consequences for misbehavior.
- Encourage children to use words to convey their feelings.
- Model cooperation, sharing, and proper behavior.
- Use soft voices with the children. Never shout.
- Show ample affection with each child.
- Expect children to help maintain the environment by having them help pick up toys and clean up messes.
- Give children the opportunity to problem solve with each other. Don't be too eager to step in.
- Anticipate problems before they happen, if possible, by being observant.

Interact and play with the children indoors and outdoors.

- Play along with the children whenever possible and involve them in household activities and routines.
- Be a good listener. Ask lots of open-ended questions and be patient with children as they speak. Spend time talking with each child every day.

Develop a partnership with the families in your program.

- Communicate regularly when family members drop off or pick up their children.
- Invite family members to become involved in your program.
- Maintain a family bulletin board with upcoming activities, parenting tips, child development information, and community resources available to them.

Maintain a well-run, organized program.

- Keep up-to-date health and emergency information files on each child in your care.
- Develop a brochure or leaflet for families outlining your center's policies, goals, services offered, and mission statement.

- Take anecdotal notes on each child.

- For each child, keep a portfolio that contains these anecdotal notes, samples of the child's art, and other evidences of skill development that can be shared with parents.

Maintain a commitment to professionalism.

- Join a national or local early childhood organization.

- Observe a strict policy of confidentiality with the families in your program.

- Continue to improve your skills by attending workshops or classes.

- Network with other family child care providers for support and exchange of program ideas and resources.

Turn to chapter 7 to prepare for the CDA exam and to chapter 8 to read about the verification visit.

Preparing for the CDA Exam

Once your CDA application is accepted, you can either complete the verification visit or take the CDA Exam. The order in which you accomplish these two tasks is your choice. However, they both must be completed within six months, and sometimes your particular state or training agency will have a shorter timeframe.

Arranging to Take the CDA Exam

This exam is not taken on your own online, but rather at a Pearson VUE Testing Center in your community. You can visit the Pearson VUE website (www.pearsonvue.com/cdaexam) to locate a center near you. The address, contact information, and even a map are provided to help you locate the center. You can schedule your exam at this same website. You will be directed to create an online account and will set up a user name and password. Make note of these so you will not forget them. You can also schedule the exam by calling Pearson VUE at 866-507-5627 (Monday through Friday, 8 a.m. to 8 p.m. EST).

After scheduling, Pearson VUE will send a confirmation note with the location and date you chose for your exam. If you need to cancel or reschedule, you can do so either by phone or by using your Pearson VUE online account. You cannot cancel within twenty-four hours of your exam. Be sure to check the location of the exam ahead of time, calculating how long it will take to get there. You need to arrive at least fifteen minutes before your appointment. If you miss your exam, it will cost $65 to reschedule.

Take along a valid photo identification card and leave your personal belongings in your car. You will be allowed one hour and forty-five minutes to complete the exam, although most candidates only need about an hour to do so. The CDA Exam is offered in both English and Spanish. If a candidate requires another language, this can be accommodated for an additional charge. The test-taking process is easy, even if you are unfamiliar with using a computer. You will be given three practice questions before the exam begins, so you can familiarize yourself with the procedures.

The entire CDA Exam is multiple choice. Many of the questions are "situational," giving you a chance to interpret an early childhood context and choose a response that is closest to the way you would respond in such a situation. The last five questions present short scenarios with a photo, and you will choose the answers that best describe your response to each of them.

The questions on this exam have been chosen to help the Council determine whether you are able to put the knowledge you have gained from your training hours into practice. The questions will be geared primarily to your particular age-group setting. So, for example, if you are an infant/toddler care provider, the questions are designed to judge your ability to apply the CDA Competency Standards in programs serving these particular children. You will take the CDA Exam: 0–3. Preschool and Family Child Care providers will take the CDA Exam: 3–5, which judges a candidate's ability to put into practice all of the CDA Competency Standards for 3-, 4-, and 5-year-old children who are in group programs. Besides these age-specific questions, the exam will also include other questions that candidates working in any setting should be able to answer.

It is suggested that you answer all of the questions, even if you are unsure of the answers, since any questions left unanswered are counted as incorrect. If you are unsure of an answer, you can "flag" that question and come back to it later. When all of the questions have been viewed, a "Review" screen will come up, showing you all of the questions that have been flagged or have been left unanswered, so you can complete them. Finally, you will click the "Submit Exam" button, which will transmit your answers to the Council for Professional Recognition to be scored.

View a tutorial about the CDA Exam at www.cdacouncil.org /storage/documents/final_ppt_CDA_Exam_tutorial.pdf.

In addition, try these seventy practice questions. Read each question and all of the answer options carefully before choosing the best answer.

You will then reflect on several early childhood situations that might occur in your particular child care setting. These are similar to the five scenarios that will be on the CDA Exam. As you reflect on what is happening in each scenario, decide on a response that represents your own knowledge and understanding of developmentally appropriate practices, not how you might be expected to respond by your supervisor. Answers to all of these questions can be found at the end of this chapter.

Practice Questions

1. The amount of adult supervision that is needed depends on
   a. the number of children in the group.
   b. the activity.
   c. the developmental needs of children who are present.
   d. all of these.

2. The first-aid kit should be kept
   a. out of the reach of children.
   b. in an easily accessible location, clearly marked, and out of the reach of children.
   c. in a restroom.
   d. in a drawer, far from where children will play.

3. Frequent hand washing is important because
   a. children need to keep hands clean.
   b. it keeps germs from spreading.
   c. it is a positive social skill.
   d. it is a law.

4. An open-ended question
   a. has one right answer.
   b. has no right or wrong answer.
   c. has two answers.
   d. has a commonly repeated answer.

5. Children should be provided with these items for washing their hands:
   a. Cold water, bar soap, and paper towels
   b. Hot water, liquid soap, and a cloth towel
   c. Warm water, liquid soap, and paper towels
   d. Water and paper towels

6. Children need their own space in the classroom for their coat and other belongings because
   a. it promotes their positive self-concept.
   b. it helps maintain good health.
   c. a and b.
   d. none of the above.

7. An example of a positive *nonverbal* communication is
   a. a smile.
   b. saying, "Good morning."
   c. ignoring a child's actions.
   d. moving away from a child.

8. At mealtime, a caregiver should
   a. insist that children finish all food on their plates.
   b. not offer any dessert until all their food is finished.
   c. only offer dessert to the children who remained quiet at the table while eating.
   d. none of the above.

9. When arranging a classroom, a teacher should
   a. keep the quiet and noisy activities together.
   b. put related activities near each other.
   c. provide a large, open area in the center of the room.
   d. arrange the furniture all along the walls.

10. The best example of an open-ended material would be
   a. an alphabet puzzle.
   b. playdough and cookie cutters.
   c. a coloring book and crayons.
   d. unit blocks.

11. The children have been asking for the same book to be read at story time every day for the past week. You will
   a. happily reread it, because you know children benefit from repetition.
   b. read a book that is similar to the one they enjoy.
   c. tell the children that they have heard that book too many times and will need to choose a new one.
   d. skip story time for a few days until they have forgotten about that book.

12. Children's play materials should be
    a. kept in closed containers.
    b. kept on low, open shelves.
    c. kept on shelves out of their reach.
    d. kept in a storage cabinet, to be taken out by the caregiver.

13. A developmentally appropriate group time
    a. lasts only a short time.
    b. gets the children actively involved.
    c. permits children to leave, if they wish.
    d. all of the above.

14. Why do you give children a warning before activities are about to change?
    a. It gives them time to clean up their toys.
    b. It provides them time to finish up an activity.
    c. It helps to quickly get their attention.
    d. It is a signal to come to the next activity right away.

15. You want children to learn the rules of conversation, so you
    a. give them practice talking, listening, and responding in casual conversation as you sit with them at the lunch table.
    b. let them know they cannot talk during lunch.
    c. tell them not to interrupt while you are talking.
    d. remind the children to use "inside voices."

16. A good early childhood practice is
    a. having the children line up to use the restroom.
    b. having the children sit outside the restroom to wait for their turn.
    c. having the children all do an art activity together.
    d. asking the children to pretend to be butterflies as they walk to the playground.

17. An activity that develops small-motor skills would be
    a. swinging.
    b. beanbag throwing.
    c. bead stringing.
    d. jumping.

18. An activity that develops small-motor skills would be
    a. manipulating playdough.
    b. walking on a balance beam.
    c. throwing a ball.
    d. riding a tricycle.

19. You have a small budget to use for purchasing materials for your classroom. When choosing, you will first consider
    a. the price and how much you can buy with what you have.
    b. the age range listed on the packaging.
    c. whether the materials are developmentally appropriate, are mostly open-ended, and will enable the children to experience success.
    d. whether the materials are familiar to the children from TV commercials.

20. Two boys want the same truck to haul blocks across the room. One boy goes to the housekeeping area and gets a basket. This is an example of
    a. an open-ended question.
    b. problem solving.
    c. a small-motor exercise.
    d. guidance.

21. When talking with a child, the caregiver should
    a. speak loudly.
    b. get down to the child's eye level.
    c. whisper softly to the child.
    d. stand and talk with the child.

22. Caregivers should
    a. control the conversations that children have with them.
    b. be good listeners.
    c. ask a lot of open-ended questions.
    d. b and c.

23. You want the children to learn cooperation, so you

    a. insist that a child let everyone play with the toy he brought for show-and-tell.

    b. discipline the children for not helping pick up the toys in the room.

    c. play a song about cooperation.

    d. provide activities that require taking turns, sharing materials, and solving problems together.

24. Children's artwork should be

    a. put on bulletin boards in the hallways.

    b. placed high on walls so other children cannot touch it.

    c. displayed at the children's eye level.

    d. put immediately into the children's cubbies to be taken home.

25. A creative arts project is

    a. marble painting on turkey shapes.

    b. painting at the easel on pumpkin-shaped paper with orange and black paint.

    c. painting with orange and black paint on white paper.

    d. sponge painting on a white ghost shape.

26. One of the children is having a tantrum just as circle time is beginning. The best way to proceed would be to

    a. stay close to the child and explain to the others that she is having a hard time right now but will be all right in a few minutes. Let your co-teacher start the circle time.

    b. call her parents to take her home.

    c. take her to the director's office until she calms down.

    d. have the child sit in the time-out chair until she can control her emotions and return to the group.

27. A creative activity is

    a. cooking using a recipe.

    b. stringing beads.

    c. using playdough.

    d. assembling a twenty-piece puzzle.

28. Which activity is creative?

    a. Using a CD that tells children how to move

    b. Dancing with scarves to an instrumental CD

    c. Using musical instruments with a CD that tells children when to play them

    d. Singing "Where is Thumbkin?"

29. A good technique for dealing with favorite toys is to

    a. provide duplicates of them.

    b. put them away when children squabble over them.

    c. provide them as rewards for good behavior.

    d. none of the above.

30. You are aware that many of the children watch a great deal of TV and videos at home. You would like the parents to support their children's development at home instead of relying on screen media. You will

    a. confront the parents at drop-off time about the detrimental effects of too much screen time for young children.

    b. send home a listing of suggested TV shows and children's videos.

    c. send home book and activity packs that the children can enjoy with their families.

    d. send home an educational video each Friday.

31. A positive circle experience includes

    a. scheduling and planning beforehand.

    b. interesting and active activities.

    c. anticipating problems beforehand.

    d. all of the above.

32. Appropriate choices for young children include

    a. "Whatever you would like to do today!"

    b. "You may have ice cream or oranges for snack today."

    c. "You may choose from art, the housekeeping area, or the puzzle table."

    d. none of the above.

33. Situations that reflect bias include

   a. Thanksgiving stories that depict Indians with war paint and headdresses.

   b. Halloween stories with pictures in which everything black is portrayed as scary.

   c. block activities that serve to exclude girls and housekeeping activities that are offered first to girls.

   d. all of the above.

34. Andrew often hits and bites other children. After doing so, he laughs and runs off. He doesn't seem to realize he is hurting them. You will

   a. isolate Andrew from the other children.

   b. ask the family to seek counseling for their child.

   c. ignore the behavior so it will not be further reinforced by your attention to it.

   d. stop the behavior immediately and attend to the hurt child. Then get down on Andrew's level, pointing out and labeling the feelings of the child he has hurt.

35. Appropriate guidance techniques would include

   a. planning to avoid problems with the use of space, placement and number of toys, and careful supervision.

   b. interacting with children in positive ways.

   c. redirecting inappropriate behavior.

   d. all of the above.

36. Fine-motor skills refer to skills that

   a. children need to move to the next developmental level.

   b. require children to work with their hands and fingers.

   c. enable children to walk on a balance beam or along a straight line.

   d. none of the above.

37. A new child has just enrolled in your program. She is from China. Several of the children have approached you to say, "Mei Lee talks funny." You will

   a. play a Chinese CD so everyone gets used to the language.

   b. explain to them that she is from another culture, speaks a different language, and is learning ours. Encourage them to help her learn our words and to be a kind friend to her.

    c. ignore their statements because they will get used to the way Mei Lee speaks.

    d. strongly suggest that Mei Lee's parents learn English. That way, they can help their daughter learn as well, and her speech will not seem different to her classmates.

38. Gross-motor skills refer to skills that

    a. require children to make large movements with their bodies.

    b. require children to participate in messy activities.

    c. require children to use scissors or eyedroppers.

    d. none of the above.

39. Children learn best when they

    a. actively participate.

    b. follow directions carefully.

    c. a and b.

    d. none of the above.

40. Marcy came to school today with an angry, negative mood. You can see that this may soon erupt into physical aggression. The best way to deal with this would be to

    a. put her into the time-out chair right away.

    b. talk to her privately and explain that she will either need to end this attitude or her parent will be called to take her home.

    c. ignore her mood, because there is also a chance it will improve shortly.

    d. provide her with an activity that will help to diffuse her angry feelings, such as working with playdough or throwing sponge balls at a target.

41. Coloring books, ABC worksheets, and offering sample artwork are

    a. activities that strengthen skills.

    b. developmentally appropriate.

    c. not developmentally appropriate.

    d. activities that should be offered every day.

42. Experience charts, labeling items in the room, and making lots of books available are all examples of

    a. practices that support emergent literacy.

    b. practices children will encounter once they begin elementary school.

    c. practices that should be provided only to older preschoolers.

    d. none of the above.

43. A writing center for preschoolers should include

    a. a variety of alphabet worksheets with letters to trace.

    b. pencils, paper, markers, envelopes, an old typewriter, and pieces of old mail.

    c. a and b.

    d. none of the above.

44. Scribbling is

    a. something that should be discouraged.

    b. an indication of a developmental delay in preschool children.

    c. an early stage in the development of children's art and writing skills.

    d. none of the above.

45. You see a coworker leaving a group of napping children alone while she goes into the hallway. You decide to first

    a. approach her personally about your concerns.

    b. go directly to the administrator and report what you saw.

    c. make note of the incident, but let it go this first time.

    d. call Child Protective Services and report this person.

46. To extend a "teachable moment,"

    a. observe what is happening.

    b. describe what is happening and ask open-ended questions.

    c. let children come up with ideas about what they would like to do.

    d. all of the above.

47. Children's artwork should

    a. be recognizable so their parents can appreciate it.

    b. emphasize the process rather than the product.

    c. both of the above.

    d. none of the above.

48. You find that it is becoming difficult to keep the children engaged during circle time. You should

    a. stop the circle time activity frequently to remind the children they need to be still and pay attention.

    b. re-evaluate the length of time you are expecting the children to stay at circle time and whether the kinds of activities you are providing are interesting to them.

    c. arrange the children so friends are not sitting next to each other.

    d. suspend circle time for a few months and then resume, seeing whether things get any better.

49. The following materials and activities are appropriate ways to help preschoolers prepare for reading:

    a. Flash cards, workbooks, worksheets, and phonics lessons

    b. Magnetic letters, a well-stocked book corner, and reading to them every day

    c. Learning the "Alphabet Song"

    d. None of the above

50. A child needs help blowing his nose. You help him use a tissue and then

    a. you wash your hands.

    b. you wash your hands and ask the child to wash his hands too.

    c. you ask the child to throw his own tissue in the covered trash can.

    d. you throw the tissue in the covered trash can.

51. Positive ways to involve parents in the program include

    a. wiping tables.

    b. reading stories.

    c. cleaning up the bathroom.

    d. all of the above.

52. You are out on the playground with twelve preschool-age children. One of the children says he needs to use the restroom, so you
    a. take the child in to the restroom, leaving the rest of the children with your co-teacher.
    b. take the child and half of the other children into the building.
    c. tell the child to wait until the class goes back into the building, because he had a chance to use the restroom before going out but did not.
    d. end the outdoor playtime and take everyone inside.

53. An important part of a quality early childhood program is for caregivers to communicate with parents. Some examples would be
    a. parent conferences.
    b. parent meetings.
    c. conversations at arrival and departure time.
    d. all of the above.

54. Parent and teacher conflicts happen. A positive way to resolve them is to
    a. practice active listening.
    b. suggest the parents look over their copy of your program's parent handbook, referring to sections that may clear up misunderstandings and address the problem.
    c. both of the above.
    d. none of the above.

55. You plan to take a walk through the neighborhood to the fire station tomorrow. To prepare for this trip, you will
    a. read a book about fire trucks.
    b. sit down and explain the trip to the children, reviewing the procedures for safely crossing the street, staying close to the teachers, and other safety rules.
    c. send home a list of field trip rules so the parents can go over them with their children.
    d. keep the trip a secret until tomorrow, because children love surprises.

56. Professional relationships with other staff include
    a. attending professional development events together, such as conferences and workshops.
    b. spending time planning cooperatively to meet the needs of the children.
    c. treating each other with respect.
    d. all of the above.

57. A milestone of development is
    a. a definite point in a child's life.
    b. a part of motor development.
    c. a functional skill or task that most children can do at a certain age range.
    d. none of the above.

58. Preschoolers will use shocking language. An appropriate response would be
    a. putting the child in time-out, isolating him or her from the rest of the children.
    b. telling the child that such language is not appropriate.
    c. giving the child a lot of attention each time he or she uses such language.
    d. all of the above.

59. A new child has enrolled who has a physical disability. So that she will feel welcome, you will
    a. make any adaptations to the indoor and outdoor environment necessary so she can fully participate in activities to the greatest extent possible.
    b. explain to the other children that she probably will not be able to do everything they can because of her disability.
    c. not make any adaptations to the environment so she will be encouraged to challenge herself.
    d. provide an aide to help her throughout the day, so you will not need to make any adaptations to the environment.

60. The purpose of observing children is to
    a. compare the growth and development among children in the group.
    b. identify patterns of their growth and development.

c. provide the teachers with information so they can plan appropriate activities for the children.

   d. both b and c.

61. Some types of observation tools are

   a. anecdotal records.

   b. running records and child interviews.

   c. developmental checklists.

   d. all of the above.

62. When you are preparing an environment for children, what should always be considered first?

   a. State licensing regulations

   b. Center policy

   c. Safety of the child

   d. CDA standards

63. You bring out a new toy fire truck for the children to play with today. The toddlers are having a hard time playing together with the truck, so you

   a. bring out a couple duplicates of this toy.

   b. put the truck away until the toddlers settle down and listen to your requests for them to share.

   c. put the truck away because the toddlers are too young to play with it nicely.

   d. ask the children to come up with a plan to take turns with the truck.

64. Classroom rules and rules for outdoor safety should be

   a. few in number.

   b. worded in simple terms, using pictures.

   c. written in positive terms, saying what the children *should* be doing.

   d. all of the above.

65. A parent has expressed concern that her son is spending too much time in your program "just playing." A good response to her concern would be to

   a. explain to her that this is what the children enjoy and what you have always done.

   b. invite her into the classroom to observe the children in order to understand what they are learning as they play.

c. provide an informational sheet that explains what children learn from participating in the various learning areas in your room as they play.

d. both b and c.

66. Child abuse and neglect reporting is the responsibility of

a. the teacher.

b. the person who observed the incident.

c. the director.

d. the social service or regulatory agency.

67. An appropriate mealtime would include

a. a well-balanced meal that meets licensing regulations.

b. pleasant conversation at the table.

c. encouragement to eat.

d. all of the above.

68. A child in your group says, "My truck!" To encourage more complex speech, you

a. say, "Is that your truck? Yes, that is your truck."

b. read a story about a truck.

c. don't respond unless he says more words.

d. put a label on his toy that reads "truck."

69. Elliot says, "Me go?" You respond

a. "Yes, you are going to the gym."

b. "I can't understand your baby talk, Elliot."

c. "No, Elliot. Say, 'Am I going to the gym?'"

d. by ignoring his grammar errors and just nodding.

70. A parent has confided in you that her husband has left her and she is upset and unsure what will happen next. The best way to proceed would be to

a. tell the other teachers in your program so they can be aware of the situation.

b. respect the parent's privacy by keeping the information confidential and offer her a list of community agencies she might find helpful at this time.

c. tell her that you would prefer not to hear about her personal problems.

d. question her son, who is in your room, about what happened with his daddy.

Preschool Practice Scenarios

1. Peggy, the preschool teacher in room 2, has been having problems keeping the children engaged during the morning. They often appear bored and some get into trouble or act out.

    I would suggest

    a. calling the parents of the children who are not behaving.

    b. observing the situation, perhaps making changes in room arrangement or the morning schedule, and providing additional activities for the children that will interest them.

    c. providing worksheets for the children to complete before they are allowed to play with the toys, so they keep busy.

    d. allowing the children to play outside instead of engaging in tabletop activities.

2. Emiko has been misbehaving all afternoon since she got up from her nap. She deliberately spilled her juice and pushed another child down outside.
    I would suggest

    a. calling her parent to take her home.

    b. taking her temperature to see whether she might be ill.

    c . reminding her of the classroom rules and providing a time-out for her.

    d. ignoring this behavior unless she seriously hurts someone.

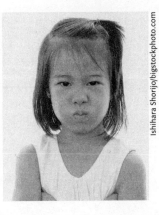

3. Melissa likes using the classroom computer. She especially likes the alphabet game and spends every morning playing it. Mrs. Harris is becoming concerned that Melissa is not taking part in the other activities in the room and is not socializing with the other children very much.

If I were Melissa's teacher, I would

a. use a timer and allow Melissa to use the computer for three minutes at a time.

b. tell Melissa that she cannot use the computer until next week, so she is forced to participate in other activities in the room.

c. take the computer out of the classroom for a while until Melissa forgets about it.

d. ask Melissa's friend, Nathan, to join Melissa at the computer. This way, Melissa will have the chance to work with and socialize with someone and still be able to participate in the activity of her choice.

Infant/Toddler Practice Scenarios

1. The infant caregiver has four infants in her room. Keeping them all happy is sometimes a challenge until her co-teacher arrives a few hours later. In the meantime, the caregiver keeps the babies in the swings. That way, she can straighten up the room and do some planning without having to worry about anybody getting hurt or into trouble.

In this situation I would

a. sit on the floor with the babies around me, so they can have "tummy time" and I can interact with them. I would wait to straighten the room until my coworker arrives.

b. place the infants in their cribs, because this would be safer and they could stretch out.

c. place the infants in infant seats with bottles of milk to keep them content until my coworker arrives.

d. place all four of the infants in a play yard together with pacifiers.

2. When the toddlers begin to get restless and lose interest in the activity she has put out on the table, Rhonda starts up a DVD they enjoy. Some of the children will watch for quite a while, and others fall asleep. The ones who won't

sit still are given a cookie and juice to settle down. If I were Rhonda, I would

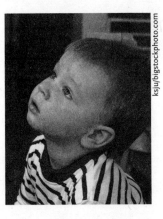

   a. continue this practice, because it seems to be working.

   b. take some time to play with the children, observing their interests. Then provide a variety of activities for them and perhaps take them outside to play when they seem bored.

   c. assume the children are tired and have them take naps.

   d. change from videos to video games, since most of the children are accustomed to playing these at home.

3. Mrs. Wilkins has asked that you not let two-year-old Maura lie down in the afternoon for naps anymore, because this is keeping her from going to bed at a reasonable time at night. However, by 11 a.m., you can see that Maura is getting tired, and after lunch, she can hardly stay awake. If you try to keep her up, she becomes cranky, cries the entire afternoon, and will not even eat her snack. You decide to handle the situation by

   a. continuing to keep Maura from napping, even though she is clearly distressed, because her parent has requested this.

   b. having a coworker take Maura for walks around the building or outside during naptime, so she does not disturb the other children who are trying to sleep.

   c. explaining to Maura's mother what happens when Maura cannot nap, and coming up with a compromise so she can rest for a shorter period of time. You might also suggest helpful bedtime routines, so Maura can fall asleep more easily.

   d. telling Maura's mother that she needs to learn better parenting skills, so her daughter will go to bed at a proper time.

Family Child Care Practice Scenarios

1. Molly has recently had several more children enroll in her family child care program. She had been telling the children to put their coats and backpacks in the spare bedroom, so they would be out of the way. However, now there are quite a few of them and it is hard for the children to find their belongings.

I would suggest that Molly

a. give each child a paper bag in which to store personal items.

b. purchase or construct simple cubbies for the children so they could store their belongings separately. I would explain that this is an important measure to ensure that germs are not being spread from one child to another.

c. spread the belongings out on a table in the garage, so they will be out of the way and the children will have an easier time locating what is theirs.

d. tell the parents that all personal belongings must be left in the car.

2. Mrs. Wilson provides art for the four-year-olds every day. She gives each of them a page from her thick coloring book and asks the children to choose two colors from the crayon box. After they finish coloring, Mrs. Wilson prints their names across the top of the page and hangs the pages on the refrigerator until the children go home. Mrs. Wilson lets the parents know if their child has done a good job staying inside the lines or if they need to work with their child on this skill at home.

If I were Mrs. Wilson, I would

a. be very satisfied that I am providing art experiences for the children and offering feedback to their parents about their progress.

b. ask the children first if they want their pictures hung on the refrigerator. They may prefer to put their pictures in their cubbies.

c. provide the children with a basket of crayons to share and large pieces of blank paper to draw on. I would also not consider "staying inside the lines" a critical skill that four-year-olds need to work on.

d. require that the children do a coloring sheet over if they scribble on it.

3. A few of the parents have expressed concern that the children were spending too much time playing and not being provided with enough academics in preparation for school. So, Mrs. Nevins now has the children sit at tables every morning to complete a worksheet about letters or numbers. The children are not permitted to leave the table to play until they finish the activity. Yesterday, one of the children began to cry, because he didn't want to work at the table any longer. Mrs. Nevins was able to encourage him to keep working and to eventually finish most of the page.

If I were Mrs. Nevins, I would

a. ask the parents to have their children complete worksheets you send home, so they get used to doing them.

b. provide stickers and other rewards to encourage the children to complete the worksheets.

c. explain to the parents that children learn through play and that requiring young children to complete worksheets is not developmentally appropriate.

d. make sure that the children are not provided their snack until they complete their worksheets.

Compare your answers with the following answer key. If you have contact with others who are working on or have already earned the CDA Credential, it would be valuable for you to discuss the questions and the scenarios in a small group for better understanding.

Answer Key to Practice Questions

1. d	11. a	21. b	31. d	41. c	51. b	61. d
2. b	12. b	22. d	32. c	42. a	52. b	62. c
3. b	13. d	23. d	33. d	43. b	53. d	63. a
4. b	14. b	24. c	34. d	44. c	54. c	64. d
5. c	15. a	25. c	35. d	45. a	55. b	65. b
6. c	16. d	26. a	36. b	46. d	56. d	66. b
7. a	17. c	27. c	37. b	47. b	57. c	67. d
8. d	18. a	28. b	38. a	48. b	58. b	68. a
9. b	19. c	29. a	39. a	49. b	59. a	69. a
10. d	20. b	30. c	40. d	50. b	60. d	70. b

Answer Key to Practice Scenarios

Preschool
1. b
2. b
3. d

Infant/Toddler
1. a
2. b
3. c

Family Child Care
1. a
2. b
3. c

Chapter 8 will help you prepare for your verification visit with the Professional Development Specialist, including the formal observation. When you spend some time reflecting and preparing, these next steps will go smoothly.

The Verification Visit

Let's assume you are ready to schedule your verification visit. You have already made initial contact with your Professional Development Specialist and have entered her identification number on your application form. You then received a Ready to Schedule Notice from the Council. You can either take the CDA Exam or schedule the verification visit first. It is your choice, but both must be scheduled within six months of receiving this notice, otherwise you forfeit your application fee, and you will need to repeat the entire CDA process and pay another application fee.

Scheduling

Getting the verification visit scheduled is easy. You will contact your PD Specialist and agree on a time to meet at your program. You will need to plan on three-and-a-half hours at minimum:

- Two hours for the observation
- Next an hour for review of your documents
- Then about forty-five minutes for the reflective dialogue

A quiet room should be made available where you and the PD Specialist can talk in private after your observation. You will make arrangements for someone to fill in for you in the classroom while you have this meeting. If there is no quiet space in your workplace, you can schedule the reflective dialogue for later in the day or on another day at a different location. Remember, however, this last step must take place within seven days.

Choose a time for your observation when the children will be active and you will be actively participating with them. This time can include meals, snacks, or any other regularly scheduled activity, as long as you are involved. You would not want your observation time to include an hour when, for example, the children go to another area of the building for a gymnastics class under the direction of another person.

Preparing for the Observation —Conducting a Self-Study

The PD Specialist will use the Comprehensive Scoring Instrument that is located at the back of your *Competency Standards* book. She will score each item on that Instrument on a scale of 1 to 3:

1 Little or no evidence of meeting the standard

2 Some evidence of meeting the standard

3 A good deal of evidence of meeting the standard

The PD Specialist will be observing the environment and also your interaction with the children. Those who have earned their CDAs often say the most valuable preparatory exercise they did was the self-study. Is this self-study really necessary? True, after completing the required professional training and work experience with young children, candidates should feel confident about their practices and the early childhood environments they provide.

However, it never hurts to participate in a little review and self-reflection! Sometimes (no, *many* times), we get caught up in the day-to-day operation of our programs and begin functioning on autopilot. Things appear to be running relatively smoothly, the children and families seem happy, and so we are too. How long has it been since you stepped back and took an objective look at what's really going on? The self-study provides just such an opportunity. It's always a good idea to be reminded about exactly what the observation will cover and that you are in compliance with every item.

The self-study serves multiple purposes. First, it offers peace of mind that you have taken a closer look, perhaps found a few things to adjust, and feel prepared. "No surprises" usually translates to "no stress." On the day of your observation, you want to be on top of your game—confident and fully functional, not impaired by nerves and fear of the unknown. You should be able to sail through that two-hour observation confident that your program and practices demonstrate an understanding of the CDA Standards and exemplify early childhood professionalism.

A second benefit of the self-study is information gathering. It may have been a while since your last self-evaluation, and there may be things that need to be fixed, changed, or improved. When we are immersed in an environment, it's often hard to see these things. Or we may have made a mental note of a few things, but they are still on the "to do" list.

A self-study can be conducted in many ways, but to make it specific to the observation at hand, we will use the CDA Competency Standards, specifically, the Comprehensive Scoring Instrument that the PD Specialist will use.

Before conducting a self-study, be sure you are fully familiar with the six Competency Standards and thirteen Functional Areas. Part 2 in the *Competency Standards* book is devoted to these.

To help you determine competency in each of the Functional Areas, the book provides Indicators and Examples. These are general in nature so that most candidates can identify with them, regardless of their particular situation. Of course, there would be more specific indicators and examples, based on each candidate's unique situation (cultural, ethnic, socioeconomic, geographical location, and family structure). When the PD Specialist conducts the observation, she may note some of these more specific indicators or examples on the Comprehensive Scoring Instrument.

You will now take a look at the Comprehensive Scoring Instrument that is located at the back of your *Competency Standards* book. You will concentrate on pages 1 through 20 of this Instrument and will not write on any part of it. These pages also go through the six Competency Standards and thirteen Functional Areas, but in a more abbreviated manner. The PD Specialist will use these pages to score your observation.

These pages are divided into three color-coded sections:

Orange: Settings and Activities
These are items in your program environment that the PD Specialist will be looking for.

Green: Actions and Interactions
The PD Specialist will use these items to score your action and interaction with the children.

Blue: Review
These are items that the PD Specialist may not be able to observe but will ask you about in order to enter a score. Or she may be able to determine your competency by checking items in your Professional Portfolio.

You can photocopy each section to take to work with you. Rate each Indicator a 3, 2, or 1, with 1 being the lowest. For every item you rate below a 3, make a note in the margin of the specific issue, your plan to remedy it, and who might be able to help you. When all three sections are completed, review your ratings and make a list of things you need to do. It may be a good idea to consult with the instructor who provided your CDA training, the center director, or your mentor for advice or assistance with any changes or adjustments you need to make.

What Happens at the Verification Visit?

You will bring your completed Professional Portfolio and the Competency Standards book to the verification visit. This meeting involves three steps, which the Council calls R.O.R.™:

1. Review
2. Observe
3. Reflect

The PD Specialist can *review,* or look over and score, your documentation (the contents of your Professional Portfolio) first or can *observe* first by conducting the classroom observation. The order of these two steps doesn't matter. However, the third step, *reflect*, must be conducted last. Since most observations occur in the morning when the children are participating in the most activities, it is probably best to plan the observation first, so none of this will be missed. When the steps have been started, all three must be completed within seven days.

Before the observation, the PD Specialist will ask you for your *Competency Standards* book so she can remove the Comprehensive Scoring Instrument from the back. She will sit in your room and proceed to go through each color-coded section, recording scores and making notes at the bottom of the pages. If you move to a different area, such as the playground, she will follow along. You should conduct your day as you usually do. Try not to make any changes in your routines or schedule. Making changes may be upsetting to the children, causing issues that will interfere with what you are doing. The more normally and naturally you can move through your day, the better your observation will proceed.

The scores you receive on the observation are combined with the scores you earned for the CDA Exam and also your Professional Portfolio in determining whether you will be awarded a CDA Credential. The PD Specialist will not be able to give you any feedback on how your observation went, but she will make note of one of your professional strengths and one area for future professional growth (a weakness that needs improvement). She will discuss these with you during the reflective dialogue, the last part of the verification visit.

During the review step of the verification visit, the PD Specialist will look over all of your documentation inside your Professional Portfolio. She will first check the My CDA Professional Portfolio, where you have checked off each item that is inside. She will also look for your signature at the bottom, indicating that you wrote or gathered the portfolio and all of its contents.

- **Proof of the Required Training.** The PD Specialist will look at the Summary of My CDA Education sheet. You will have initialed each of the eight listed subject areas, indicating that you completed at least eight hours of training in each one of them. She will then look at your training certificates and transcripts, making sure they represent 120 clock hours and were awarded by an accepted agency or organization.

- **Family Questionnaires.** Next, the PD Specialist will look at the Family Questionnaires Summary Sheet, checking to see that you have recorded the number of questionnaires distributed and collected. She will count your questionnaires, making sure the numbers match. The PD Specialist will not read the questionnaires.

- **The Reflective Competency Statements.** Each of these statements will be read. If something was unclear during the observation, the PD Specialist uses what you have written in these statements to determine whether you have met a particular standard.

- **The Resource Collection.** Each item will be checked, making sure you have collected what was required.

  Two items will be checked very closely during this review: if you do not have the documentation for your 120 clock hours of training or have training that is not accepted by the Council and a current first-aid/CPR certificate that meets all requirements, you cannot earn your CDA Credential until these are corrected. The PD Specialist will wait until the end of your verification visit to tell you if either of these two problems exist and to explain that the Council will be sending a postcard with the required procedures. This must be completed within six months of the date you received the Ready to Schedule Notice.

- **The Professional Philosophy Statement.** The PD Specialist will read this statement, looking for evidence of how you put your philosophy into practice. She will talk about these during the reflect step of the verification visit.

  Based on the observation and review of your Professional Portfolio, the PD Specialist may ask you a few questions about items on the Comprehensive Scoring Instrument that she was not able to read about or observe.

Next will be the reflective dialogue, the last step of your verification visit. At this point, all of the scoring has been completed. Now there will be a casual conversation between you and the PD Specialist, none of which will be scored.

You will be using the CDA Verification Visit Reflective Dialogue Worksheet in the back of your *Competency Standards* book. You will have already filled in boxes A and B with Area(s) of Professional Strength and Area(s) for Future Professional Growth, as identified by the families in your program on the Family Questionnaires. You will reflect on these with the PD Specialist. Then you will do some self-reflection, jotting down a couple strengths and areas for improvement in boxes C and D that you can identify in yourself. Since you will not be doing this until you meet with the PD Specialist, it is a good idea to start thinking about these strengths and areas needing improvement now, so you are prepared and not caught off guard. On paper, write down your thoughts about these questions:

- What do you see as your greatest areas of strength as an early childhood professional?

- How do you think you were able to develop these strengths?

- What do you think are areas that need improvement or further professional development?

- Why do you think these areas are more challenging for you than your strengths?

Because you thought about these questions ahead of time, you will be less likely to draw a blank when the PD Specialist asks them during the reflective dialogue.

Next the PD Specialist will share with you one area of strength and one area needing improvement that she noted about you during the observation or when she reviewed the contents of your Professional Portfolio. This should be accepted as constructive criticism and you should not take offense. It is only by receiving this kind of objective feedback that we can improve on our practices and grow as professionals in the field of early childhood. The PD Specialist will also comment on your Professional

Philosophy Statement. She may ask you to explain how you put the ideals indicated in your philosophy into practice as you work with young children. You may want to read through each part of your Professional Philosophy Statement prior to the verification visit, thinking of some examples so you are prepared to respond. For example, if in one part of your philosophy you stated that you believe young children learn best through hands-on activities, be ready to explain the types of activities you provide for them that support this part of your philosophy.

The back side of the worksheet has spaces where you will be setting goals for yourself, based on the strengths and areas for future growth that were identified. The PD Specialist will not specify any goals for you but will encourage you to set three goals for yourself. More often than not, if a person sets her own goals and commits to meeting them, they will be achieved. No one can do this for you! However, you can always ask for help as you strive to reach your own goals.

The PD Specialist will brainstorm with you to come up with a plan for reaching each of the goals you set. She will then encourage you to share these goals with a person you can count on for support and encouragement, such as a supervisor, instructor, mentor, or coworker. This person should be someone who will keep you motivated to improve and commend you when you reach your goals.

Finally, at the bottom of the worksheet, you commit to achieving the goals you have set and sign your name. Your PD Specialist will also sign as witness to your commitment. This worksheet is yours to keep, so you are reminded of the goals you set and can check them off as they are met. This concludes the verification visit.

Chapter 9 will explain how the CDA Credential is awarded and what steps to take if it's not. You'll also find suggestions for continuing your professional development as a lifelong learner.

Award of the CDA Credential

When the verification visit has concluded, you will need to wait for a response from the Council. A majority of the time, this response will be in the form of receiving your CDA Credential in the mail.

Sometimes a candidate does not meet the Council's criteria for the CDA Credential for one reason or another. In those situations, the Council will send a letter indicating this and will offer the candidate the opportunity to appeal the decision, as well as providing information about what happens next.

This letter will *not* indicate for what reason specifically the candidate did not meet CDA Standards. In other words, it will not say that a candidate answered too many questions wrong on the CDA Exam, or there was something amiss during the observation, or the Professional Portfolio had some incorrect items. Instead, the Council will only tell the candidate in which of the seventeen Functional Area(s) she showed some weakness.

Because this is such a generalized response, to prepare for another attempt at the verification visit and a CDA Credential, the candidate will need to review all of her documentation, revising and making improvements where necessary. It may be wise to let an early childhood professional, perhaps someone who has already gone through the CDA process, look over the materials and provide some suggestions. In many cases, you may be able to appeal the Council's decision. For example, if you feel that you needed some special assistance during the exam or verification visit or that the PD Specialist did not act professionally or otherwise violated policies, you may be entitled to another verification visit. Call the Council for information about filing an appeal. If you do not qualify for an appeal, you will need to repeat the CDA process and pay another application fee. You can, however, use the same training hours that you listed the first time.

Where Do You Go from Here?

Completing the CDA process and being awarded the CDA Credential is commendable. It shows your commitment to professional excellence in working with young children. However, it doesn't have to end here. You are now in a unique position to continue on your path of professional development by getting your degree in early childhood education. The field of early childhood education is changing, as new research continues to unlock new information about how young children grow and learn. It is an exciting time to be in our profession, and earning your CDA is only the beginning.

If you took courses toward your CDA from an accredited college and earned college credits, you can use them toward your degree. In fact, you can probably continue your course of study with the very same institution. You may want to get an associate's degree, which is a two-year program. Many two-year community colleges have articulation agreements with four-year institutions within the same state. So upon completing the two-year degree, you are able to move into the four-year program as a junior. You may, at that point, decide you want to teach in an elementary school or beyond. Or you may want to continue in your work with children under the age of five. In any case, after only two additional years, you would earn your bachelor's degree.

Paying for additional education does not have to be a roadblock to your future. Many of the state scholarship agencies that were available to help you with your CDA training now have funding in place to assist with degree programs as well. Check with the particular agency you worked with or the child care resource and referral agency in your community for current information about scholarship funding. The college you attend will also be able to help you through its department of financial aid.

Through the CDA process, you have proved your competence and ability to conquer new challenges that lie ahead. Don't let anything or anyone stand in the way of your goals and aspirations. It is always best to continue your education right away. The longer you wait, the more likely you will be to find excuses and give other things priority over your professional development goals. Plan to contact your local community college this week to get information to start working on your degree. You owe it to yourself and to the young children and their families who depend on you.

Chapter 10 will provide you with the information you need to renew your CDA Credential, which must be done within an allotted amount of time. You will also learn how to get a CDA Credential for a different setting, if you have experience in a setting other than the one you used for your initial CDA Credential.

CDA Renewal and Earning a CDA Credential for a Different Setting

10

Earning a CDA Credential indicates that you have achieved recognition in the early childhood profession based on your competency in working with young children and their families. Your CDA Credential can be kept as part of your professional preparation and qualifications indefinitely, as long as it is renewed when required.

More than likely, you spent one or two years in the CDA process taking classes for the required training hours, writing the Competency Statements, assembling the Professional Portfolio, taking the CDA Exam, and finally being observed and participating in the verification visit with the PD Specialist. If you allow your CDA Credential to expire, you will lose what you worked so hard to attain.

If it is not renewed within the allotted time limit and your CDA Credential expires, you will have to begin the process all over. No one wants to let that happen, but every year many people do. With a little foresight, commitment, and a calendar, this can easily be avoided.

The CDA renewal process allows you to reaffirm your competence, as well as to acknowledge your affiliation with early childhood professionals who are dedicated to providing quality care for young children.

How Often Must My CDA Credential Be Renewed?

Your CDA Credential needs to be renewed before the third-year anniversary date for every renewal. There is no longer a five-year renewal or any grace period provided. All CDA renewals are for three years. Let's say your CDA Credential was issued on October 7 three years ago. If your renewal application is received on October 8, just one day past the three-year anniversary date, you are, as they say, a day late and a dollar short!

The Council has said that if you provide a valid e-mail address, the Council staff will send a renewal reminder. However, it is not a good idea to depend on anyone to remind you to renew your CDA. You should keep track of the expiration date and make a note to yourself to renew. Better safe than sorry!

Getting a Renewal Packet

To receive a renewal packet, you can do one of two things:

1. Call the Council (1-800-424-4310) to request one.

2. Order online at www.cdacouncil.org.

You may remember having experienced a long wait for your original *Competency Standards* book after it was ordered. This may have been due to a high volume of requests, a back order, or some other warehouse problem. Keep in mind that this could also happen when ordering your renewal packet. Allow plenty of time before your CDA expires to order and receive your renewal packet, fill out the application, assemble the required documentation, and get everything sent back to the Council. We suggest that you allow at least three months. You cannot apply to renew, however, more than sixty days before it expires.

What's in the Renewal Packet?

When you receive your renewal packet, it will contain these items:

1. **The CDA Renewal Application Form** The top part of the form is to be filled out by you. The bottom part is to be completed by the Early Childhood Education Reviewer. This will be a person you know who is familiar with your work with young children and who meets specific experience and educational requirements set by the Council. These requirements are explained later.

2. **A CDA Renewal Procedures booklet**

3. **A booklet of information for the Early Childhood Education Reviewer**

4. **Waiver Request forms**

5. **A listing of national early childhood membership organizations**

What's Involved in the Renewal Process?

Renewal is actually a seven-step process:

STEP 1. *Select an Early Childhood Education Reviewer to complete a Letter of Recommendation to enclose with the application*

You will ask someone to be your reviewer who has firsthand knowledge within the past year of your skills and abilities working with young children. This person can be a coworker, a center director, an early childhood coordinator, or a member of an early childhood organization to which you belong. The person you choose must have training in early childhood education or child development and have direct experience with programs for young children. Specifically, she must meet all of the requirements in *one* of these three categories:

1. A bachelor of arts, bachelor of science, or advanced degree in early childhood education/child development or home economics/child development from an accredited college or university, including twelve semester hours covering children ages birth through five years. In addition, the individual must have two years of experience in a child care setting serving children ages birth to five years. During this time, one year needs to have been spent as a caregiver or teacher working directly with children in the same age range as the children in the candidate's classroom and one year must have been spent being responsible for the professional growth of another adult.

2. An associate-level (two-year) degree in early childhood education/child development or home economics/child development from an accredited college or university, including twelve semester hours covering children ages birth through five years. The individual must also have four years of experience in a child care setting in a program serving children birth through five years. During this time, two years must have been spent as a caregiver or teacher working directly with children in the same age range as the children in the candidate's classroom and two years must have been spent being responsible for the professional growth of another adult.

3. An active CDA Credential, including twelve semester hours of study in early childhood education or child development at an accredited college or university covering children ages birth through five years. This individual

will also have six years' experience in a child care setting serving children ages birth to five years. During this time, four years must have been spent as a caregiver or teacher working with children in the same age range as the children in the candidate's classroom and two years must have been spent being responsible for the professional growth of another adult (Council for Professional Recognition 2013).

In addition, your relationship with the reviewer cannot constitute a conflict of interest. Examples of such conflicts of interest would include a person who was your coworker in the same classroom, a person related to you by blood or marriage, or a relative of one of the children in your classroom. Any of these situations would be considered a conflict of interest and would interfere with the reviewer's objectivity and credibility.

The Council will consider waiving certain requirements if the potential reviewer has other qualifications or experience. The potential reviewer must submit a written explanation and documentation of alternative formal and informal training related to early childhood education and child development and experience in early childhood teacher preparation. The Waiver Request form is included in the CDA renewal packet or available for download in the Resources section of the Council's website (www.cdacouncil .org). This form may either be sent in by mail or fax:

The Council for Early Childhood Professional Recognition
2460 16th Street NW
Washington, DC 20009-3575
fax: 1-202-265-9161

(You may also use the Waiver Request form if you are substituting some of the required documentation or don't have quite enough experience hours but have a valid excuse.)

The person acting as your reviewer will be expected to read the CDA Competency Standards and thirteen Functional Areas in the *Information for the Early Childhood Education Reviewer* booklet. After doing so, she will complete the recommendation form, also found in this booklet. The form asks the reviewer how long she has known you and in what capacity. The reviewer will then check one of the following choices:

- I strongly recommend this CDA for renewal.

- I recommend this CDA for renewal.

- I recommend, with reservations, this CDA for renewal.

The reviewer is given space on the form (and can also use a separate sheet, if desired) to describe your performance with children in relation to the six CDA Competency Standards and the thirteen Functional Areas.

Finally, the reviewer will sign the form, as well as complete some identifying information. The form will then be returned to you in a sealed envelope. The reviewer will also need to fill out and sign the bottom half of your CDA Renewal Application Form (Council for Professional Recognition 2013).

STEP 2. *Show proof of current first-aid certification*

You will need a current Red Cross, Green Cross, American Heart Association, or local hospital pediatric first-aid certificate. You will enclose a photocopy of the certificate with your application.

STEP 3. *Show proof of 4.5 continuing education units (CEUs) or a 3-credit-hour course or 45 clock hours*

One CEU is earned by ten contact hours of participation in an organized continuing education experience under responsible sponsorship, capable direction, and qualified instruction. And 4.5 CEUs equal forty-five contact hours of instruction.

You may obtain CEUs through participation in several types of training, including in-service and association-sponsored workshops. However, to be accepted, these training sessions or workshops must award CEUs. They must be documented in the form of a certificate or transcript issued by an agency or organization with expertise in early childhood teacher preparation. College coursework and CEUs may be obtained at vocational/technical schools, community colleges, or two-year and four-year colleges and universities. Check with the Council about other types of clock hours that will be accepted. The policies about acceptable clock hours are changing.

To meet this requirement, all coursework must be in early childhood education or child development and should cover one or more of the following eight subject areas:

1. Planning a safe, healthy learning environment

2. Steps to advance children's physical and intellectual development

3. Positive ways to support children's social and emotional development

4. Strategies to establish productive relationships with families

These training hours must have been earned since you obtained your CDA Credential and not be part of your initial CDA training. You will send a photocopy of a college transcript, your CEU certificates, or proof of clock hours with your application.

5. Strategies to manage an effective program operation

6. Maintaining a commitment to professionalism

7. Observing and recording children's behavior

8. Principles of child growth and development

These training hours must have been earned since you obtained your CDA Credential and not be part of your initial CDA training. You will send a photocopy of a college transcript or of your CEU certificates with your application. All CEUs and college coursework must have been completed within the past five years (Council for Professional Recognition 2013).

Step 4. *Show Active Status as a Caregiver*

To revalidate your CDA Credential, you need to have maintained your competency in working with young children. Therefore, you are required to maintain a current relationship with young children even if you no longer work directly with children. Within one year prior to your renewal, you must have a minimum of eighty hours of work experience with young children. If your employment no longer involves working with young children, there are other ways of meeting the requirement. These might include spending time in an early childhood setting as a helper or volunteer.

To verify the hours you have worked, have someone familiar with your work (preferably a supervisor) write a letter of confirmation. This letter will be submitted with your application form and other documentation. The person you ask to do this could be a coworker, a lead teacher, a center director, or someone in a similar role (Council for Professional Recognition 2013).

Step 5. *Show Proof of Membership in a National or Local Early Childhood Professional Organization*

You are required to be an active member of a national or local early childhood association. CDAs are expected to demonstrate basic knowledge about young children and their families. They are expected to conduct themselves in an ethical manner at all times. The requirement for CDAs to belong to professional organizations has been in effect since 1996. A list of such organizations is provided in the CDA Renewal Procedures booklet and also in the Resource Center link on the Council website (www.cdacouncil .org/resource-center). You will enclose a photocopy of your membership card or other document proving that you have been a member during the past year prior to your application for renewal (Council for Professional Recognition 2013).

Step 6. *Collect All Documentation and Completed Forms, Along with the Renewal Fee.*

The Renewal Fee became $100 as of September 1, 2013.

Step 7. *Mail Everything to the Council.*

We suggest sending these materials via certified mail, return receipt requested. That way, you will not only have proof of mailing but will also receive a card indicating that your envelope was received. You will mail it to this address:

> The Council for Early Childhood Professional Recognition
> 2460 16th Street NW
> Washington, DC 20009-3575

An alternative to mailing in an application is applying online using YourCDA on the Council's website. If you use this option, the renewal fee is $75. You will first make sure you have met all the requirements for renewal (steps 2 through 5). Then you will obtain a valid e-mail address from the person who will vouch for your CDA renewal (your Early Childhood Education Reviewer). An e-mail request for this person to submit an online recommendation will be sent from the Council as part of the online application. You can pay the renewal fee online using a credit card. After registering and submitting your application using YourCDA, you will mail in the required documentation (steps 2 through 5) to the Council at the address listed. If you prefer to pay the renewal fee by check or scholarship, this can also be sent in with your documentation (Council for Professional Recognition 2013).

What Happens After the Council Receives My Renewal Application?

When your renewal application has been received, the Council will review your materials. If the materials you sent are *incomplete* (perhaps you forgot to enclose something), the Council will notify you and you'll have the opportunity to correct the problem. Since this will obviously delay your renewal for months, it's best to double-check that everything is in order and completed before mailing in your materials. The Renewal Procedures booklet has a handy checklist for everything you'll need to send in along with your application form. *Use it!*

If everything *is* complete and all requirements are met, the Council will award the CDA Renewal Credential, which is valid for another three years. When you receive it, mark your calendar as a reminder for your *next* renewal, so it won't be overlooked.

Earning a CDA Credential for a Different Setting

Some people want to earn a second CDA Credential for a different setting. To do this, the candidate must complete the credentialing process again for this new setting (family child care, center-based preschool, or center-based infant/toddler) and submit a new application fee. To satisfy the 120 clock hours of professional education, the candidate can reuse parts of the training she listed for the first CDA setting, if the content also relates to the second setting. An example would be a class about health and safety, which would be general in nature, relating to both settings. On the other hand, classes relating specifically to a certain age group, such as "Curriculum for Preschoolers," could not be used for an Infant/Toddler CDA Credential (Council for Professional Development 2013).

CDA Subject Areas for the 120 Clock Hours of Training

Within the past five years, CDA candidates must have completed 120 clock hours of formal child care education, with at least ten hours in each of the eight subject areas listed here. This requirement may be met through participating in a variety of options available, including in-service training and coursework at a college or university. The examples provided will help you determine which of the subject areas have been covered by a training session or course and how many clock hours were devoted to each. This breakdown will need to be indicated on the Direct Assessment Application form.

Subject Areas	Examples
1. Planning a safe, healthy learning environment	Safety, first-aid, health, nutrition, space planning, materials and equipment, play
2. Steps to advance children's physical and intellectual development	Large- and small-muscle development, language and literacy, discovery, art, music, mathematics, social studies, science, technology, dual-language learning
3. Positive ways to support children's social and emotional development	Adult modeling, self-esteem, self-regulation, socialization, cultural identity, conflict resolution
4. Strategies to establish productive relationships with families	Parent involvement, home visits, conferences, referrals, communication strategies
5. Strategies to manage an effective program operation	Planning, record-keeping, reporting, community services
6. Maintaining a commitment to professionalism	Advocacy, ethical practices, workforce issues, professional development, goal setting, networking
7. Observing and recording children's behavior	Tools and strategies for objective observation and assessment of children's behavior and learning to plan curriculum and individualize teaching, developmental delays, intervention strategies, individual education plans
8. Principles of child development and learning	Typical developmental expectations for children from birth through age five, individual variation including children with special needs, cultural influences on development

Title of Course or Training	Total # Clock Hours	Subject Areas							
		1	2	3	4	5	6	7	8

Sample Observation Tool (Anecdotal Record Form)

There are several types of observation tools that can be used to record information about a child's behavior. Among them are checklists, time samplings, running records, and anecdotal records. Item RC V of the Resource Collection asks that you locate and use an observation tool to observe and document a child's developmental/learning progress. If you do not have one of your own, you might want to use an Anecdotal Record form like the sample form that follows.

An *anecdotal record* is a type of observation tool. It is a short, written record based on observation of a child's behavior. It is recorded during the course of the day while the child is engaged in his regular schedule of activities. An anecdotal record is a snapshot, taken at one point in time, recording what was seen and heard, usually no more than one or two paragraphs in length. These notes include dates, times, and the context in which the observation was conducted (for example, indoors or outdoors, area of the classroom, with whom, engaged in what activity).

Anecdotal records are quite valuable during parent-teacher conferences, when the teacher needs to explain how a child is doing and why. These records also help to justify why the teacher made a particular decision regarding a child and to plan appropriate activities to support his or her development.

To maintain validity, credibility, and value, anecdotal records must be entirely objective. The purpose of these records is to document behavior, not to provide comment or opinion on it. After completing the observation, there is typically a space at the bottom of the form, separate from the observation recording area, where the observing teacher can make notes and express an opinion or comment, if desired. Look over the completed example, to clarify your understanding of an anecdotal record.

Choose a child to observe in your program. Be as inconspicuous as possible while recording the information about what you see and hear so the child will not be influenced by your presence. Do *not* indicate the child's name on the form. Write only what you see and hear. Do not include any personal feelings, opinions, or comments. Save those for the section at the bottom.

Observation Tool
Anecdotal Record

Date	Context	Child
September 20	Housekeeping Area with 2 other girls, playing restaurant.	M. (female) age 3

Time	Observation
9:30 a.m.	M. enters the Housekeeping Area where L. and D. are playing restaurant. M. says, "Can I play, too? I can be the waiter or the cooker." D. answers, "Sure. You can help us cook the eggs." M. proceeds to get out some pans and spoons. She watches what D. is doing and imitates her. The 3 girls continue playing together for about 5 minutes. M. leaves to paint at the easel. NOTES: M. is making good progress in entering a play situation without being disruptive. She asked if she could join the girls this time, instead of barging into the area and taking over.

C

Sample Activity Plan Form

Use this activity form template for all nine of the activities that you plan for Resource Collection item RC II.

Type of activity: ....

Name of activity: ....

Intended for age: ....

Goal for this activity: ....

Materials:

....

....

....

Procedures:

....

....

....

This activity is developmentally appropriate
for this age group because

....

....

....

Sample Weekly Activity Plan for Infants

The sample form shows one day's worth of activities. You will need to create five days of activities, one for each day of the week, for one infant.

Weekly activity plans for infants are decidedly different from those used for groups of toddlers and preschoolers. This is because caring for infants is highly individualized and the curriculum revolves almost exclusively around their care and routines. Therefore, the sample form provided reflects the activity plan for one specific infant, rather than for all of the infants in the group.

In actual practice, the care provider would complete one of these forms for each infant in her care. The activity sections reflect the major areas of development. Spaces for regular daily routines such as napping, diapering, and feeding are also included so specific information about the child's day can be recorded.

For Resource Collection item RC I–3, you are asked to provide a sample of a weekly plan you would use with your group of children. As an infant/toddler caregiver, you may either provide a weekly plan for infants or you may provide a weekly plan for toddlers, depending on the age group you work with predominantly. If you would prefer a weekly plan for toddlers, see appendix E for a sample.

Besides listing appropriate activities and goals, you are also asked to indicate the adaptations necessary for children who may have special needs.

You may use your own activity plan form or the blank form provided in Appendix C. Since you will be using a weekly activity plan for one specific infant, you will complete it for a child with special needs, either actual or fictitious.

At the top of the sample Individual Weekly Activity Plan for Infants are spaces for the child's first initial and a very brief description of her disability. In the boxes you will indicate specific activities and the learning goals associated with them. You will also describe how you will adapt each activity to enable this child (who has some type of disability) to experience, learn from, and enjoy these activities to the maximum extent possible. For ideas about adapting activities for children who have special needs, you will find the following websites helpful:

The Center for Inclusive Child care (inclusivechildcare.org)

Tots 'n Tech (tnt.asu.edu)

National Network for Child Care (www.nncc.org)

Individual Weekly Activity Plan for Infants

Name: K. (female) 8 months
Date: April 6–10
Special Need(s): Developmental delays (low neck and upper body strength)

Monday

Language Development

Activity: Story: *Baby Faces* by Margaret Miller

Say words that name parts of the faces and point to them

Learning Goals: Hearing the names of parts of the face

Adaptation: None needed

Cognitive Development

Activity: Drop the Toy

Take turns dropping the toy to the floor and watching it drop

Learning Goals: Object permanence

Adaptation: Hold K. in lap to keep her in upright position

Creative Development

Activity: Crib Gym

Suspend toys over K.'s feet. Encourage her to kick and move them

Learning Goals: Make objects move with her feet

Adaptation: None needed

Gross Motor

Activity: Tummy Time

Place K. on her tummy. Place toys within her reach

Learning Goals: Raise her head and upper body, reach for toys

Adaptation: Play for short periods of time so she doesn't tire

Fine Motor

Activity: Picking up Cheerios on Tray

Learning Goals: Grasping with her fingers

Adaptation: Extra support

Social Development

Activity: Saying Hello

Place K. on tummy face to face with a friend

Learning Goals: Encourage responses

Adaptation: Play for short periods of time so she doesn't tire, place her on her back and talk with the teacher, and make faces

Sample Weekly Activity Plan for Preschoolers and Toddlers

The sample form shows one day's worth of activities. You will need to create five days of activities, one for each day of the week, for a toddler or preschooler.

For Resource Collection item RC I–3, you are asked to provide a sample of a weekly plan you would use with your group of children. You may use your own form or one of the samples provided here. One is for toddlers and the other is for preschoolers.

The information on the form must include brief descriptions of the activities provided for each of the learning areas. You will need to describe the expected learning goals for each activity, as well as the ways you would adapt the activity for a child who has special needs.

You may have a child with special needs in your classroom. If so, you will indicate, briefly, the nature of the disability on the form. To maintain confidentiality, do not use the child's name. Instead, use the child's first initial. For each activity, you will suggest how you could make adaptations that would enable this child to learn, experience, and enjoy it to the maximum extent possible.

If you do not have a child with special needs in your classroom, you will need to create a hypothetical child who has a disability. On the form, you will indicate the child's particular disability and then describe how you would adapt your activities for that child. For ideas about adapting activities for children who have disabilities, check out the following websites:

The Center for Inclusive Child care (inclusivechildcare.org)

Tots 'n Tech (tnt.asu.edu)

National Network for Child Care (www.nncc.org)

Weekly Activity Plan for Toddlers

Theme: Bubbles
Children with Special Needs: M. has small-motor and sensory impairment.
Date: April 4–8

Monday Activities

Playing with Toys and Materials

Activity: Exploring Bubble Plastic

Under supervision, press and stand on bubble plastic of different sizes

Learning Goal(s): Find out what happens when the bubbles are pressed

Adaptations: Use a block for pressing bubbles

Exploring Art

Activity: Painting on Bubble Plastic

Large brushes on pieces taped to the table, may make prints

Learning Goal(s): Dip brush in paint, brush paint on plastic, enjoy process

Adaptations: Use Velcro fastener to attach brush to hand, assist

Music and Movement

Activity: "Bubbles, Bubbles All Around"

Song/movement sung to "Twinkle, Twinkle, Little Star"

Learning Goal(s): Follow movement directions in the song

Adaptations: Assist with movement instructions

Dramatic Play

Activity: Blowing Bubbles with Our Puppet Friends

Puppets, soft plastic bubble wands, small plastic pails: pretend to blow bubbles

Learning Goal(s): Remember how we blew bubbles and repeat this with the puppets

Adaptations: Assist with using the puppets

Water, Sand, and Other Media

Activity: Bubbles in the Water Table

Use baby shampoo; include small plastic boats, funnels, and sieves

Learning Goal(s): Sensory experience of the bubbles

Adaptations: Provide small tub for bubbles

Story Time/Language/Literacy

Activity: Story: *Bubbles, Bubbles* by Kathi Appelt

Read the story together, talk about the pictures

Learning Goal(s): Identify the body parts that are mentioned in the story

Adaptations: Provide a board book version of this book

Outdoor Play

Activity: Blowing Bubbles

Use rings and large wands, hula hoop

Learning Goal(s): Dip wand, blow or wave, enjoy the process

Adaptations: Wands with Velcro-fastener attachments

Food and Tasting

Activity: Bubbly Apple Juice

Prepare apple juice using sparkling water

Learning Goal(s): Sensory experience of carbonated juice

Adaptations: None required

Weekly Activity Plan for Preschoolers

Theme: Caterpillars
Children with Special Needs: M. has sensory and small-motor impairment.
Date: April 4–8

Monday Activities

Circle Time

Activity: Story: *The Very Hungry Caterpillar* by Eric Carle

Flannel board Story: Give each child a story piece to add to the story

Learning Goal(s): Recognize the right time in the story to add a particular piece to the board

Adaptations: Assist with placement of piece on board

Art

Activity: Bouncing Caterpillars

Dip inflated balloons in paint and bounce them on large paper to make caterpillars

Learning Goal(s): Hold balloon, dip in paint, and make prints

Adaptations: Use clothespin as a handle

Music and Movement

Activity: "The Little Caterpillar"

Sung to tune of "Itsy Bitsy Spider"

Learning Goal(s): Learn the words, tune, and movements to the song

Adaptations: Assistance with movements

Dramatic Play

Activity: Becoming Butterflies

Caterpillar and butterfly costumes, items of food that the caterpillar ate in the Eric Carle story

Learning Goal(s): Retell the story by acting it out, using costumes and props

Adaptations: Assistance with costume

Science

Activity: Observing a Butterfly

Monarch butterfly caterpillar in our Butterfly Box

Learning Goal(s): Understand the life cycle of this butterfly by observing over time

Adaptations: None required

Math

Activity: Butterfly Count

Count out plastic butterflies to place in cocoon baskets labeled with numbers 1 to 5

Learning Goal(s): One-to-one correspondence with objects and numerals

Adaptations: Use larger plastic butterflies

Outdoor Play and Gross-Motor Development

Activity: Caterpillar Crawl

Crawling through a fabric tunnel

Learning Goal(s): Learn concept of fast and slow as they crawl through the tunnel

Adaptations: None required

Fine-Motor Development

Activity: Find the Butterflies

Reach in and pull only the butterflies out of a cloth bag cocoon

Learning Goal(s): Discriminate the butterfly shapes from the caterpillar shapes

Adaptations: Use larger shapes

Language/Literacy

Activity: Story: *The Very Hungry Caterpillar* by Eric Carle

Read the story together, talk about the pictures

Learning Goal(s): Follow the life of a caterpillar, predict what will happen next

Adaptations: Give M. the board book version of this book

Professional Philosophy Exercise

Reflect on the following statements as you think about your beliefs regarding early education. Try to write at least a paragraph for each one as you work through the statements. This exercise will help you organize your thoughts and prepare to compose your CDA Professional Philosophy Statement.

In chapter 1, I suggested that you begin on this right away, even before you fully complete your training hours or write your Reflective Statements of Competence. Then don't look at it again until you are nearing the end of your CDA journey.

When your Professional Portfolio is complete, reopen this exercise and prepare to be amazed at how much you have changed. Parts of this exercise may stay the same, but you will revise others based on the new understanding and experiences your training and work with young children have provided since you wrote your initial responses.

After you finish your revisions, you will be ready to write your document for the Council.

Complete these statements:

- My personal understanding about children and learning include

....

....

....

- I believe the purposes of early childhood education are

  ....

  ....

  ....

- I think that children learn best when

  ....

  ....

  ....

- The curriculum of any early childhood program should include certain "basics" that support a child's emotional, social, physical, and intellectual development. These basics are

  ....

  ....

  ....

- I believe children learn best in an environment that promotes learning. A good learning environment would have such features as

  ....

  ....

  ....

- All children have certain basic needs that must be met if they are to learn and develop in the best ways possible. Some of these basic needs include

  ....

  ....

  ....

- I would meet these needs by

  ....

  ....

  ....

- A good teacher should have certain qualities and act in certain ways. Qualities I think are important for teaching include

  ....

  ....

  ....

- When we teach, we not only consider the children, but also their families. I know it is important to make families part of what I do because

  ....

  ....

  ....

- Students who have special needs often require adaptations in instructional practices to meet their needs. Some strategies I can use to help me teach children who have disabilities include

  ....

  ....

  ....

- Early childhood professionals work with children and families from diverse cultural backgrounds. There are many ways teachers can provide for children's learning styles while responding appropriately to diversity. Modifications I could employ to create a more culturally responsive learning environment include

  ....

  ....

  ....

You have now completed this exercise. Open this up again after your training and your Professional Portfolio are completed and use what you have written here to compose your Professional Philosophy Statement.

Glossary

bilingual specialization The CDA applicant can request to be assessed for a bilingual specialization. The applicant must work in a program in which the adults and children use the two languages consistently and simultaneously. The applicant must also be able to speak, write, and read both languages.

candidate A person who has met all eligibility requirements and has applied for CDA assessment. The candidate compiles the necessary documentation, distributes and collects Family Questionnaires, and participates in a verification visit conducted by the Professional Development (PD) Specialist.

Center-Based Infant/Toddler One of the setting choices for CDA assessment. This is a state-licensed child development center where a provider works with a group of at least three children. All of the children in the group are ages birth through thirty-six months.

Center-Based Preschool One of the setting choices for CDA assessment. This is a state-licensed child development center where a provider works with a group of at least eight children. All of the children in the group are ages three through five.

Child Development Associate (CDA) This is a person who has successfully completed the CDA assessment and has been awarded the Child Development Associate (CDA) Credential™. A CDA has demonstrated competence in meeting CDA standards through her work with young children in a center-based or family child care program. A CDA is capable of meeting the needs of children in a developmental context, and she works to support their physical, emotional, social, and cognitive growth. A CDA has also shown the ability to effectively work with families and other adults.

clock hour A clock hour is 60 minutes.

Code of Ethical Conduct Standards of ethical behavior that have been developed by the National Association for the Education of Young Children (NAEYC) for the early childhood education profession.

competence The ability or skill to do something well.

Competency Standards The Competency Standards specify the skills and goals that a competent early childhood care and education provider will be able to demonstrate in working with young children. There are six CDA Competency Standards:

I. To establish and maintain a safe, healthy learning environment

II. To advance intellectual and physical competence

III. To support social and emotional development and to provide positive guidance

IV. To establish positive and productive relationships with families

V. To ensure a well-run, purposeful program responsive to participant needs

VI. To maintain a commitment to professionalism

Comprehensive Scoring Instrument The multipage form found at the back of the *Competency Standards* book. This is used by the PD Specialist to score the Professional Portfolio and the formal classroom observation.

continuing education unit (CEU) A unit is awarded for participation in a sponsored, continuing education session conducted by a qualified instructor. The session is not for credit, and each unit is equivalent to ten contact hours of study. When a candidate wishes to renew a CDA, 4.5 CEUs are required, which is equivalent to forty-five contact hours of study.

credential A written document that shows that a person has met specific standards. The Council awards the CDA Credential to caregivers who have demonstrated competence in the CDA Competency Standards.

developmental context Each of the Functional Areas includes a developmental context, or summary, of children's development and for working with children at different stages of development.

dual-language learners Children whose primary language is one other than English. They may be learning their own language simultaneously with English or may be learning a second language in addition to their primary language.

endorsement An endorsement is determined by the ages of the children in a candidate's care. If a candidate is working in a center-based program, she has a choice between preschool (three through five years old) and infant/toddler (birth to thirty-six months). Family child care providers are assessed on their work with children who may range in age from birth through five years.

Family Child Care One of the setting choices for CDA assessment. A family child care home is one that meets at least the minimum level of state and local regulations where the candidate can be observed working with at least two children who are five years old or younger, who are not related to the caregiver.

Family Questionnaires Forms that are distributed to the parents and guardians of the children in a candidate's program, which enables families to describe their perspective and evaluation of the candidate's work. The candidate uses this feedback to reflect on child care practices and to set professional development goals.

Functional Area The six CDA Competency Standards are divided into thirteen Functional Areas that further define a caregiver's work with children.

Professional Development (PD) Specialist An experienced early childhood professional who has completed the required training modules, passed the online exam, and been certified by the Council for Professional Recognition to conduct verification visits.

Professional Portfolio An organized compilation of documentation and personal reflections that demonstrates the candidate's eligibility to be awarded a CDA Credential, based on the CDA Standards. The portfolio consists of five sections, including documentation of the candidate's professional education (training certificates/transcripts), the Family Questionnaires, the Resource Collection, the six Reflective Statements of Competence, and the Professional Philosophy Statement.

reflective dialogue The final part of the verification visit, when the candidate and PD Specialist converse about the candidate's reflection on areas of strength and areas for professional growth, resulting in setting professional goals and developing strategies for implementing them. This part of the verification visit is not scored and will not figure into the final credentialing decision.

renewal The process by which an expiring CDA Credential is revalidated. The Credential must be renewed the first time by three years after the date it was awarded. Subsequent renewals will be every three years as well.

setting The type of child care program in which the CDA candidate is working and will be observed by the PD Specialist. The three settings include center-based preschool, center-based infant/toddler, and family child care.

specializations There are several specializations candidates may want to add to their CDA Credential:

- Bilingual, for candidates working in programs in which two languages are spoken consistently
- Monolingual, for candidates working in programs in which a language other than English is spoken
- Special Education, for candidates meeting the requirements for either center-based or family child care who are working primarily with children who have special needs.

verification visit A scheduled meeting of the candidate and the PD Specialist at which time the candidate will be observed working in a program with young children. The PD Specialist will also review the candidate's Professional Portfolio, and the two will engage in a reflective dialogue.

waiver(s) The Council will sometimes excuse certain eligibility or information collection requirements for a PD Specialist or a candidate. A request for a waiver must be submitted on a Waiver Request Form.

References

Bailey, Caryn T. 2004. The 2004 National Survey of Child Development Associates (CDAs). Survey results report prepared in collaboration with the Council for Professional Recognition and the Center for Research on the Education of Students Placed at Risk. Washington, DC: Howard University.

Bureau of Labor Statistics. US Department of Labor. *Occupational Outlook Handbook,* 2012–13 edition.

Council for Professional Recognition. 2006. *The Child Development Associate Assessment System and Competency Standards for Family Child Care Providers.* 2nd ed. Washington, DC: Council for Professional Recognition.

Council for Professional Recognition. 2010. *The Child Development Associate Assessment System and Competency Standards for Infant/ Toddler Caregivers in Center-Based Programs.* 3rd ed. Washington, DC: Council for Professional Recognition.

Council for Professional Recognition. 2011. *The Child Development Associate Assessment System and Competency Standards for Preschool Caregivers in Center-Based Programs.* 3rd ed. Washington, DC: Council for Professional Recognition.

Council for Professional Recognition. 2013. *The Child Development Associate National Credentialing Program and CDA Competency Standards.* Infant-Toddler Edition. Washington, DC: Council for Professional Recognition.

Council for Professional Recognition. 2013. *The Child Development Associate National Credentialing Program and CDA Competency Standards.* Preschool Edition. Washington, DC: Council for Professional Recognition.

Council for Professional Recognition. 2013. *The Child Development Associate National Credentialing Program and CDA Competency Standards.* Family Child Care Edition. Washington, DC: Council for Professional Recognition.

Council for Professional Recognition. 2013. *Essentials for Working with Young Children.* Washington, DC: Council for Professional Recognition.

Index

renewal, 13, 167–174
state recognition, 3
training subject areas, 4–5
types of endorsements and settings, 6–10
verification of training, 6
verification visit, 155–161
CDA Exam, 133–154
family child care setting practice scenarios,
151–154
infant/toddler practice scenarios, 150–151
practice questions, 135–148
preschool practice scenarios, 149–150
scheduling exam, 13, 133
test taking tips, 134–135
time line for, 13, 155
CDAs. *See* Child Development Associates (CDAs)
CDA Verification Visit Reflective Dialogue
Worksheet, 31, 160–161
center-based program directors
Competency Standards book and, 19
CDA Credential for, 20
functional area self-study tips, 21–25
questions about CDA verification visit, 18–20
supporting CDA candidate, 17–18, 25–26
center-based programs
overview of, 8
PD Specialist CDA verification visit, 18–19
See also infant/toddler setting; preschool setting
Center for Inclusive Child Care, 182, 184
CEUs (continuing education units), 5
for renewal process, 171–172
challenging behavior, children with, 51, 84, 118
child abuse and neglect, reporting, 44–45, 77, 111–112
Child Care Services Association, 6
child care settings. *See* family child care setting;
infant/toddler setting; preschool setting
Child Development Associate (CDA) National
Credentialing Program, 1–2
Child Development Associates (CDAs)
defined, 1
demographics of, 2
See also CDA Credential
circle activities
family child care setting, 129
infant/toddler setting, 93
program tips, 62
classroom environment. *See* Learning Environment,
Functional Area 3
clock hours
bilingual setting, 9
for CDA Credential, 4–5, 10, 18
documentation of, 58, 91, 125, 159
for renewal process, 171
sample form, *176*

for second setting credentials, 174
subject areas, 4–5, 175
verification visit and, 159
Code of Ethical Conduct (NAEYC), 55, 58, 88, 91, 122
Cognitive, Functional Area 5
family child care setting, 114–116
infant/toddler setting, 80–82
preschool setting, 47–49
program director self-study items, 23
program tips, 61, 95, 128
college courses
recommended topics, 5
Communication, Functional Area 6
family child care setting, 114–116
infant/toddler setting, 80–82
preschool setting, 47–49
program director self-study items, 23
program tips, 96
community agencies. *See* agencies
Competency Standards
center-based program directors and, 19
defined, 11
Competency Standard I
family child care setting, 102–104, 112–114
infant/toddler setting, 68–69, 78–80
preschool setting, 35–37, 46–47
Competency Standard II
family child care setting, 104–107, 114–116
infant/toddler setting, 70–72, 80–82
preschool setting, 37–40, 47–49
Competency Standard III
family child care setting, 107, 116–119
infant/toddler setting, 72–73, 82–85
preschool setting, 40–41, 49–51
Competency Standard IV
family child care setting, 108–109, 119–120
infant/toddler setting, 73–75, 85–86
preschool setting, 41–43, 52–53
Competency Standard V
family child care setting, 109–110, 120–121
infant/toddler setting, 75–76, 86–87
preschool setting, 43, 53–54
Competency Standard VI
family child care setting, 110–112, 121–122
infant/toddler setting, 76–77, 87–89
preschool setting, 43–45, 54–55
Competency Statements, 11
family child care setting, 102–112
infant/toddler setting, 68–77
preschool setting, 34–45
verification visit and, 159
Comprehensive Scoring Instrument, 156
self-study using, 156–158
use and review of, by PD Specialist with candidate,
13, 18